Your Towns and Cities in the G

Yateley
in the Great War

Your Towns and Cities in the Great War

Yateley
in the Great War

Peter J. Tipton

Pen & Sword
MILITARY

First published in Great Britain in 2018 by
Pen & Sword Military
An imprint of
Pen & Sword Books Ltd
Yorkshire – Philadelphia

ISBN 978 1 47387 652 1

A CIP record for this book is available from the British Library

Printed and bound in England
by CPI Group (UK) Ltd, Croydon, CR0 4YY
Typeset in Times New Roman
by Aura Technology and Software Services, India

Pen & Sword Books Ltd incorporates the imprints of
Pen & Sword Archaeology, Atlas, Aviation, Battleground, Discovery,
Family History, History, Maritime, Military, Naval, Politics, Railways,
Select, Social History, Transport, True Crime, Claymore Press,
Frontline Books, Leo Cooper, Praetorian Press, Remember When,
Seaforth Publishing and Wharncliffe.

For a complete list of Pen & Sword titles please contact

PEN & SWORD BOOKS LIMITED
47 Church Street, Barnsley, South Yorkshire, S70 2AS, England
E-mail: enquiries@pen-and-sword.co.uk
Website: www.pen-and-sword.co.uk

Or
PEN AND SWORD BOOKS
1950 Lawrence Rd, Havertown, PA 19083, USA
E-mail: Uspen-and-sword@casematepublishers.com
Website: www.penandswordbooks.com

Contents

Finchampstead

Berkshire

Sandhurst

Yateley

River Blackwater

Eversley

+ St Peter's

Darby Green

Frogmore

Royal Military College Sandhurst

Staff College

Yateley

A30

Blackwater

Frimley

+ Holy Trinity

Hawley

Surrey

Hampshire

Minley
+ St Andrews

Elvetham

Hawley with Minley

M3

London and South Western Railway

Farnborough

South Eastern Railway

Cove

Royal Aircraft factory

Aldershot

Yateley Society

Charles Weager

Yateley and surrounding civil parishes, names and boundaries in the First World War. Note that the M3 and some major roads have been added for locational purposes to assist the modern reader.

– – – Denotes parish boundaries in the First World War.

Preface

From its formation in 1981, the Yateley Society has created exhibitions on themes of local history, planning matters and ecological topics. A cumulative understanding has been built up over the years of the environmental and social forces which have shaped the community over the past 500 years. In 2014, for the centenary of the outbreak of the Great War, the Society staged an exhibition in the local library. It had taken the best part of two years' research to shape this exhibition, which focussed only on 1914. The original plan was to continue the sequence in each centenary year of the Great War.

Having started researching 1915, we quickly realized that a book could impart much more of what we were discovering to a much wider audience. The Yateley Society is a registered charity whose 'area of benefit' is the Civil Parish of Yateley. We set out to discover how the First World War village coped with the traumas and exigencies of war, and how the consequences of war began to shape the town we live in today. We therefore approached Pen & Sword with the idea that Yateley, a town today but in the Great War a village of fewer than 500 houses, might fit into their new *Towns & Cities in the Great War* series.

With a contract, a new target and a deadline, the project team expanded and met monthly to discuss progress with research, and to determine the content of the book. As a civic trust, our focus would be on the home front. The Society's Chairman was adamant throughout that the research was being carried out for its own sake, whether it was included in the book or not: all would be archived for future use. Graham Fleuty, one of our team, had already published

Yateley Men at War, Heartbeats of Remembrance. Having visited all the battlefields on the Western Front, Graham tells the story of each man remembered on Yateley War Memorial, their military backgrounds and the circumstances in which each met his untimely death. Readers wanting military history should consult his book along with this one.

Members of the team chose their research topics. Muriel Brent chose the village school which she had attended in the 1930s. She was ably assisted by Graham Sargent. Philip Todd researched the Red Cross hospitals, because one ward of the Yateley hospital was actually in Eversley. Charles Weager had researched Belgian refugees for the 2014 exhibition, and then went on to research the village as a military training area under Aldershot Command. He has also hand-drawn our maps based on the 1910 Land Tax Assessment. Jerry Camp decided to research the food chain: from the local shops, pubs and farms, to the local allotments and rationing. Roger Coombes and Alan Stuckey looked at the Town Council's records, while the late Ken Walters extended his previous research on the Baptist communities in Yateley. Based on her oral history research, Valerie Kerslake wrote an article describing the character of the village before, during and after the First World War.

Other members of the team contributed essential information we needed. Chris Willis transcribed the 1914 and Spring 1919 electoral registers, and created an interactive map from the 1910 Land Tax assessments previously transcribed by Richard Johnston. Barry Moody transcribed the 1911 census, as well as researching our many naval men. Although there appear to be few descendants still living in Yateley whose families lived here during the Great War, both Chris Bunch and Robin Strange could tell us about their fathers. Chris has a particularly extensive collection of documents and photographs.

Acknowledgements

The Society has to thank all those who have willingly allowed us to use as illustrations their postcard collections, photographs and documents. The core of the Society's image library was amassed by the late Sydney Loader, one of the Society's first Vice Presidents, and then Jean McIlwaine significantly added to it when she was Church Archivist. Gordon Harland, Richard Johnston, Malcolm Miller, Philip Todd and George Trevis have private postcard collections. We must particularly thank all those family historians around the world who have contacted us, and continue to contact us. We acknowledge their specific contributions in our bibliography.

Peter Tipton had created the 'Yateley Community' on *Lives of the Great War*, the Imperial War Museum's permanent digital memorial to all those throughout the old Empire who were involved in the First World War. His aim was to connect all the military and civil records of each man and woman from Yateley who served in uniform during the war to their 'Life Story' page on the IWM website. He has already identified over 500 persons. With such a wealth of information, Peter volunteered to pull the whole story together and write the text for the book.

All proceeds and commissions which would normally be due to the author will accrue to the Yateley Society, registered charity no.282397.

Roger I. Coombes, Chairman   Peter J. Tipton

Introduction

In the early 1600s, Yateley men were being mustered as non-professional soldiers, just as their Territorial Army successors would be at their annual training camps on the eve of the Great War. Scanning down the rolls of men attending the muster on 6 September 1625, a familiar surname, Shakespeare, catches the eye. Not *the* Shakespeare, just a namesake. John 'Shackspeere' was mustered as a 'muskettere' for Mr Beverly Britten who lived at Yateley Hall (then known as Calcotts). In 1914, in a remarkable coincidence of symmetry, another Shakespeare lived in Yateley. William Shakspeare was living at Yateley Hall Farm. He was the local Hampshire County Councillor, and he and his family will play a prominent role in our story of the Great War. There had been no other Shakespeares living in Yateley in the intervening 300 years.

The name William Cave also connects the 1625 muster with Yateley in the First World War. In 1625, William Cave lived in Monteagle House, then known as Brickhills. He was Clerk to the Auditor for Wales; today we would call him a senior civil servant. He had to provide one-third of a musketeer for the 1625 muster. On 13 September 1918, his direct male heir, William Sturmy Cave, was awarded the DSO for gallantry whilst serving with the 2/4th Battalion of the Hampshire Regiment at Havrincourt in France. In 1914, F company of the 4th Hants was based at the Drill Hall in Yateley. Captain Cave's father was Colonel Sir Thomas Sturmy Cave KCB, who had joined the Yateley Volunteers just after the unit had been founded in 1860 by Captain George Mason of Yateley Manor.

Perhaps it was the centuries of military tradition in Yateley, perhaps the proximity to Sandhurst and Aldershot, or perhaps it was because

Marriage of William Shakspeare to Sheila Marion Kirkpatrick at St Peter's, Yateley,
on 23 April 1913. All the village girls were invited to be bridesmaids. Father of the
bride was Brigadier General William Johnston Kirkpatrick. The groom was a major
in the 3rd (Reserve) Battalion, North Staffordshire Regiment. His father, also William
Shakspeare, was a director of Messrs James & Shakspeare of the London Metal
Exchange, and County Councillor for Hartley Wintney Rural District. The groom's
mother organized the local committee to support Belgian Refugees. (Jean McIlwaine)

some of the principal residents, like George Mason, had fought in the
Napoleonic Wars which caused the residents of Yateley to take such
a robust view of the perceived threat of invasion by Napoleon III in
1860. Whatever the reason, Yateley was one of the first villages in
Hampshire to form a volunteer company, and this one event was crucial
in determining one of the key roles Yateley would play in the Great War.

During the Haldane Reforms of 1906-1912, which transformed
the Army's Volunteer Battalions into the modern Territorial Army,
Sir Thomas Sturmy Cave had been one of the key advisors to the
War Office. In 1920, when Yateley War Memorial was erected in a
prime position on the green opposite Yateley's parish church, it was
the daughters of George Mason who gave part of their front garden
to be its site.

Yateley's War Memorial does not cover the whole civil parish,
and the extent of the civil parish in 1919 was not exactly the same

as it is today. For the modern reader, some explanation is needed of the two neighbourhoods within Yateley Civil Parish and the character of its near neighbours.

Our account of Yateley in the Great War will cover the Civil Parish of Yateley as it was then, and will explain why the 4th Battalion of the Hampshire Regiment played such a large part, and why so many of the names on the Yateley War Memorial served in that battalion. To explain why, when war was declared, there were also so many Yateley men already serving in the regular Army, or who were immediately called-up as Reservists, we must look at local geography and the population of immediately neighbouring towns and villages.

Yateley and its Neighbours
Yateley is a parish in the far north-east corner of Hampshire, now bounded by the River Blackwater to its north and the A30 to the south. From medieval times, the ancient parish had been much larger in area, with three tithings: the village of Yateley (called the Inner Tithing) and the two outer tithings of Hawley and Cove. In the nineteenth century, both Hawley and Cove had become new ecclesiastical parishes, with their own new churches. In medieval times, Minley was in a different Hundred from Yateley, but was still included in Yateley parish. From Saxon times, Hampshire was divided in Hundreds, which were replaced by District Councils in 1894. After 1894, Minley was part of the Civil Parish of Hawley.

A few miles east of Yateley on the A30 were the Royal Military College in Sandhurst, Berkshire, and the Staff College in Camberley, Surrey. Today, the whole site is the Royal Military Academy, and the Staff College has relocated. A few miles to the south-east of Yateley are Farnborough, where Colonel Cody made the first manned flight in Britain in 1908, and Aldershot, the 'Home of the British Army'. With such close military neighbours, it could be expected that the people of Yateley would play a significant role in the Great War.

Surrounded by urban expansion, most of it military, Yateley was slowly changing, but in 1914 it would have appeared to be a small rural village dominated by large mansion houses. Yateley still

The Scene of Mr Cody's Fatal Accident. Mays. Aldershot 80.

Colonel Samuel Franklin Cody had been the first man to fly an aeroplane in Britain, on 16 October 1908. On 7 August 1913, he was flying his new Cody Floatplane with Hampshire cricketer William Evans as a passenger. The plane had been designed and built by Cody as an entrant in the Daily Mail *Circuit of Britain Race. The plane suffered a structural failure at 200ft. Cody and Evans, who were not strapped in, were both killed. An estimated 100,000 people attended Cody's funeral in Aldershot. (Malcolm Miller)*

retained the characteristics of the scattered heathland settlement it had always been, although it had greatly shrunk to just over 3,000 acres when its ancient tithings had been hived off as separate parishes. As in medieval times, the main community would still have appeared to be the buildings lining the common land we now call Yateley Green. The parish church, the manor house and the inns lie at the eastern end of Yateley Green, which then widens into a large expanse of common land to the west.

Away from this historical core, large mansions had been built, most having their own home farms and cottages for their staff. We shall look at these in some detail because the families who owned them dominated both the war effort on the home front and provided the officers and nurses serving on the front lines. Many of their gardeners and stable lads served as 'other ranks'.

Within the civil parish, the small hamlets of Cricket Hill, Darby Green and Frogmore lie where there has always been land good enough to cultivate. Each hamlet had its pubs and small shops.

The position of the new Cricket Pavilion was decided by George Higgs, proprietor of the White Lion and a keen cricketer. This illustration shows the opening ceremony in 1909. The pavilion was built on Yateley Green, now registered common land. The modern Tithings stands on its footprint. (Jean McIlwaine)

The area of the parish was then 3,222 acres, of which about one-third was Yateley Common, poor heathland on which armies had trained and held manoeuvres for centuries. In the past this heathland had extended much further, all over the ancient parish of Yateley, and well into Surrey, Berkshire and other nearby parishes of Hampshire. It was this vast tract of heathland, then commons, which attracted the Army to establish its headquarters at Aldershot in 1854. Most of the common land in the region was gradually requisitioned to provide land for barracks, ranges and manoeuvres. Although Yateley Common was used extensively by the Army, none of it was purchased by the Government until they acquired Minley Manor in 1936.

In 1851, Aldershot and Farnborough were tiny hamlets with populations of 875 and 477 respectively; by 1911, the Urban District of Aldershot had a population of 20,155, and Farnborough had 14,199. Aldershot, 9 miles from Yateley, was the largest town in this area of Hampshire, the larger town of Reading being only 12 miles away in Berkshire. Camberley owes its existence to the

The main Exeter Road crossing Yateley Common, westbound after leaving Blackwater. Known as the Hartford Bridge Flats in the First World War, the common was completely devoid of trees, making it ideal for infantry training. (Jean McIlwaine)

establishment of the Royal Military College at Sandhurst in 1812, built in Berkshire exactly where the three counties of Berkshire, Surrey and Hampshire meet. The community which grew up to service the RMC was established along the old coaching road to Exeter. In 1911, the parish of Frimley with Camberley had a population of 13,673. Just 4 miles away from Yateley church, Camberley was Yateley's nearest town with comparable shopping and banks, but was then only two-thirds the size of Yateley today.

During the First World War, Yateley's population (1,879) was similar to that of Hawley (1,736) but smaller than Hartley Wintney (2,172) and Odiham (2,674), and much smaller than Sandhurst (3,265). Fleet (3,281) had already been created an Urban District in 1904. Of the parishes surrounding Yateley, only Eversley (841) and Finchampstead (866) were smaller.

The Civil Parish of Yateley itself was essentially a parish of two halves, the dividing line being decided differently by different institutions, as still happens today. The national census divided the parish east and west of Cricket Hill: western Yateley was called 'the village' and had a population of 892; the eastern half, which included Frogmore, Darby Green and Starve Acre, had a slightly larger population of 987.

The ecclesiasical authorities placed the dividing line differently. By an Order in Council gazetted on 15 March 1901, numbers eighty-one to 109 on the schedule of the 1901 census within the Civil Parish of Yateley were transferred to the Ecclesiastical Parish of Holy Trinity Hawley. These properties transferred to Holy Trinity can conveniently be called Frogmore, as they included two of Yateley's five largest mansion houses, Frogmore Park and Hurstleigh. Today, Darby Green lies in the recently created Ecclesiastical Parish of St Barnabas. During the Great War, this hamlet was in the Parish of St Peter's Yateley, although it did already have its own 'tin church' on Darby Green.

During the First World War, the Post Office authorities chose to give all houses in Yateley the postal address of 'Yateley Camberley Surrey', and this continued until the 1990s. But in the First World War, the Post Office gave the houses in Frogmore, Darby Green and Starve Acre just their street address or house name, followed by 'Blackwater Camberley Surrey', or sometimes just 'Camberley, Surrey'. This is very confusing for anyone searching military records for men who lived in Hampshire in the eastern part of the Civil Parish of Yateley, as the postal address was used for most records, and most men stated their address as 'Blackwater, Camberley, Surrey' or just 'Camberley, Surrey'. As this book covers the Civil Parish of Yateley in the Great War, we should confirm at the outset that the number of Yateley men killed in the war was far higher than those on Yateley's War Memorial. The forty-two names on the memorial were associated with families only in St Peter's Ecclesiastical Parish

The Prelude to War
The story of any community is the story of the families who have lived there. The buildings in which they lived, worked, learned and relaxed provide the continuity to the story of the community over time, because the families living in the houses, or using the buildings, change over time. Those living in the community collectively create

institutions to enable and order community life. Governments impose institutions and laws for national and regional purposes. In a time of war, local people will find that national interests have taken over their lives. The Great War was a time of great change. In the small village of Yateley, some families who were living in Yateley in 1914 had moved away by 1919, so the names of their loved ones are not recorded on Yateley's memorials. The story of *Yateley in the Great War* is best anchored in the buildings in which families either continued to live, or moved into and out of during the war.

The story of *Yateley in the Great War* is told in these terms: the families, the buildings and the local institutions in which they were educated, worshipped, left behind to serve on the war front, or to serve as volunteers to sustain the war effort.

Little Croft, built before the First World War on Handford Lane, was replaced by a cul-de-sac of modern houses at the bottom of Tudor Drive. John Hautenville Cope and his wife E.E. Thoyts rented the house in 1910. They both contributed to the Hampshire edition of the Victoria County History *published in 1911. During the Great War, Mrs Agnes Edith Gulland, a widow, lived there. Her two sons were Army officers. She placed an obituary in the* Reading Mercury *after Captain John Perfect Gulland of the 69th Punjabis was reported killed. Luckily, he survived as a Prisoner of War. This postcard was sent on 23 December 1913 by Hugh Gardner to his mother in Hankow, China. He boarded at Little Croft throughout his schooldays until he joined the RAF in 1918 as a Cadet Pilot. (Malcolm Miller)*

A volume of the Victoria County History for Hampshire was published in 1911. This provides a short contemporary description of Yateley, but only mentions six buildings: the Manor House, Yateley Hall, Frogmore Park, Monteagle Farm, the parish church and the Dog & Partridge Inn. Four sets of historical records for the years 1910 and 1911 provide an ideal starting point to analyse the houses and their occupiers in the Edwardian heyday before the outbreak of the Great War. These four are the 1911 census, the 1910 Land Tax Assessment, Kelly's Directory and the Ordnance Survey map.

Of the thirty largest houses in Yateley in 1911, twenty-three still had their original occupants living in them in 1914. These twenty-three houses represent only 7 per cent of the total of 440 occupied dwellings in the civil parish. Because many of these large houses also had lodges, inhabited stables, gardeners' cottages and other estate houses for their employees, these mansions dominated life in the parish by their physical presence, the employment they provided, the customers they represented to local tradesmen, the farms they owned and the leading roles assumed by their families in parish governance and affairs.

The 1911 census, the latest to be released under the 100-year rule, was the first census completed by the householders themselves, recording the number of rooms in the house as well as all the usual details of their families. Kelly's Directory of 1911 divides these heads of households into three categories: private residents (the gentry), commercial (tradesmen and farmers) and the rest whom Kelly's does not list. The assessment for the 1910 Land Tax describes each house in great detail, listing the uses of each room, and even the state of repair of the whole building. A copy of the 1910 Ordnance Survey was heavily annotated by the Land Tax assessors, enabling modern researchers to locate each house exactly and to see which land was then being divided up for future development.

The picture of the village as it prepared for the possibility of war is very complete, and provides the *dramatis personae* for the opening scenes of *Yateley in the Great War*.

Houses and Families before the War

Anyone attending school in the 1950s might believe that the operation of the Elizabethan Poor Laws, with its settlement certificates, had resulted in populations of English rural villages remaining static, with little movement of families over three centuries. In 1905, in his *History of Crondall and Yateley*, the Vicar of Yateley devoted an appendix to examining the surnames found in church and manorial documents over the centuries, and concluded that twenty-one surnames had survived from seventy years previously. He noted that at least three surnames had survived in the parish since a survey of 1287: White, Heath and Wolwrich (surviving as Wooldridge). Watts is a fourth surname still surviving today from the thirteenth century.

In reality, local historians tracing the history of Yateley's houses find that the surnames of their owners and occupiers rarely survived more than two or three generations. This is partly because houses were sold to new owners, and partly because of the inheritance rules of manorial copyholdings, a medieval form of land tenure which survived in Yateley until 1925. If there was no direct male heir to a copyholding, then a daughter would inherit, sometimes all daughters jointly. The largest landed estate in Yateley, Hall Place, is a good example of a property which remained in the same family but through female inheritance. Sir Richard Ryves, a member of the Court of Committees of the East India Company, acquired Hall Place in 1668, and Lord Arundell, a direct descendant, who had acquired it via his wife's inheritance, sold it in 1820, then calling it Yateley Manor. In the meantime, the estate had been three-times inherited by female inheritance, changing the surname of the owner from Ryves through Helyer and Wyndham to Everard-Arundell.

After the Dissolution of the Monasteries in the 1530s, the Dean & Chapter of Winchester continued to own the Manor of Crondall as a source of income. Unlike an aristocrat or squire living in a grand house in other communities, the Dean & Chapter did not seem to mind who lived in Yateley, or how often property changed hands. The more times it changed hands, the greater was their income. Families came and went, improving their lot or falling into hard times. By 1914, families in Yateley had mostly only lived here for a maximum of two generations. Older properties were still changing hands and enterprising local developers were starting to buy manorial fields to build new houses. This subdivision of fields is recorded by the tax assessors on the maps accompanying the 1910 Land Tax records. Throughout the Great War, property was still changing hands, and after the war the process of changing ownership and property development accelerated.

It should also not be overlooked that this era was a time when houses and land were held as a sound investment. Consequently, most properties in Yateley were occupied by tenants, often on a short-term rental, sometimes from absentee landlords. There are even several instances of men owning one property in Yateley as tenants of the Ecclesiastical Commissioners and living in another house as a tenant of another tenant of the commissioners.

It is thus Yateley's houses which provide the continuity to its history, rather than long-established families. A house built on a particular site may not be the exact same house which stood

The four daughters of Richard Lyon Geaves and his wife Janet, née Chute Ellis. (Jean McIlwaine)

there when the Dean & Chapter of Winchester were forced by their tenants to draw up the *Crondal Customary* in 1567 to list all dwellings and tenants in Yateley. The ancient houses may have been extended, elegantly refronted or even demolished and completely rebuilt, but the site of habitation is continuous. Local people today can still recognize the sites of those old houses because the modern housing estates, now replacing many of these demolished old houses, often still bear their names. Of the six First World War mansions described in detail below, three have been demolished for modern development.

Yateley Manor

A good example of a new house built on an old site is Yateley Manor, the largest landed estate recorded in the 1567 *Customary*. In 1914, the Manor House was not the large medieval house of 1567. In 1828, a London tea dealer had pulled down that house and replaced it with the building which is still part of Yateley Manor School. During the Second World War, the house ceased being a family residence, and after the war part of its large manorial estate became known as Manor Park, the first large development of post-Second World War council houses.

In 1914, the process of change was continuing. Captain Richard Lyon Geaves owned the Manor House, with some of the lands and cottages still remaining from its medieval holdings. He had purchased the estate from Captain George Mason, who had started the 'Yateley Volunteers' in 1860. Richard Lyon Geaves had served in The Prince of Wales' Own West Yorkshire Regiment, resigning his commission in October 1881. Having played football for the Old Harrovians and Clapham Town, he had even managed to play one international match for England. By 1914, he was still holding the ancient Manorial Court of Hall Place to regulate the tenancy of his houses, but he had already sold off much of the medieval land holdings. In recent years he had sold fields to local developers to create new housing such as Coronation Road. But on 9 March 1914, he leased the Manor House itself to Sir Charles Stewart-Wilson.

A tableau vivant *performed by seven ladies at Minley Manor. The photograph is from the Geaves' family collection. Two of the sisters served as VADs (Voluntary Aid Detachment nurses) at the Minley Military Hospital in the First World War. (Jean McIlwaine)*

View of the Manor House from its lawns. Captain Richard Lyon Geaves, the owner, leased the house and grounds to Sir Charles Stewart-Wilson, who bcame a senior civil servant in the new Ministry of Munitions. (Malcolm Miller)

Yateley Manor, South Aspect.

Sir Charles had recently returned from serving at the highest levels of the Indian Civil Service, retiring as the Indian Director General of Posts and Telegraphs. The Manor House then had thirteen bedrooms, a bathroom, four reception rooms, a conservatory, kitchen, pantry and servants' hall. The market value of just the Manor House and the 46 acres of the parkland leased by Sir Charles was assessed at £4,846. Having arrived back in England from India, Sir Charles became a member of the government committee set up to organize the British Telegraph Service, and then, at a crucial time for the government in 1915, he was appointed Assistant Secretary in the newly created Ministry of Munitions. He retained this post until 1921 and lived at Yateley Manor throughout the Great War.

Although Yateley Manor had, from medieval times, been the largest landed estate in the ancient parish, the owner at one time also owning Minley Manor and the old coaching inn called the Red Lion at Blackwater, in 1914 it was no longer the largest house in the civil parish.

Frogmore Park

Of the thirty houses in the 1911 Yateley census having ten or more rooms, only two were in Frogmore and Darby Green. The Honourable Gertrude Fitzroy lived at Frogmore Park and retired Admiral Herbert William Sumner Gibson lived at Hurtsleigh, just off the main London Road we now call the A30. Both houses had a Camberley postal address and were in the ecclesiastical parish of Holy Trinity, Hawley. Indeed some of Admiral Gibson's land and most of its fourteen tied cottages were in Hawley Civil Parish. Nevertheless, the census and the Electoral Registers record both large houses and their occupants in the Civil Parish of Yateley.

Lady Gertrude Fitzroy was the widow of Horatio Fitzroy, who had died in 1900. He was directly descended from Charles II, the 3rd Duke of Grafton having been his grandfather. Lady Fitzroy was the daughter of Lord Feversham. The Fitzroys had purchased Frogmore in the early 1860s and brought up two sons and four daughters. The eldest daughter was still living with her in 1914. The eldest son was Sir Almeric Fitzroy, Clerk to the Privy Council. It was over his signature that the proclamation of war was issued in

Frogmore House was the home of the Honourable Gertrude Fitzroy. During the Great War, her son Sir Almeric Fitzroy was Clerk to the Privy Council, residing at the Fitzroys' London property in Belgrave Gardens. Frogmore House was demolished after the Second World War. (Jean McIlwaine)

August 1914, in the name of King George V. Despite the fact that Sir Almeric owned a large house in Wiltshire, he often spent his weekends hunting and shooting over Yateley Common. During the working week he lived at the Fitzroys' fashionable London address, a fifteen-room house at 55 Lower Belgrave Street.

Lady Gertrude was very involved with charitable work in London. She was Honorary Secretary of The Fitzroy Club for Working Lads. At the age of 87, on 8 May 1914, to raise funds for this charity, she organized two performances at the Royal Court Theatre of a play written by her granddaughter, Yvonne Fitzroy, and Douglas Tollemache Anstruther. Yvonne Fitzroy, the only daughter of Sir Almeric, also took a leading part in the play. The fact that Lady Fitzroy was very well connected to the aristocracy is apparent from the Royal Court programme, which lists her organizing committee and the patronesses. The latter include two duchesses, two marquesses and fourteen countesses.

The 1911 census records Frogmore Park as having twenty-six rooms, the highest number in Yateley. The assessment for the 1910 Land Tax states that it was an 'old fashioned residence brick built and with tiled roof in moderate repair'. The description lists 'drawing room, dining room, library, sitting room, boudoir, servants hall, housekeepers room, butler's room, kitchen and usual offices, 8 bedrooms, 2 dressing rooms, 8 servants bedrooms and a boxroom'. There was a greenhouse, farm buildings, stabling for four horses, a cottage in the grounds and two lodges. The market value of the whole estate was estimated at £12,042, which included a valuation of the house of £6,308. The house was demolished after having been requisitioned for Canadian troops during the Second World War.

Hurstleigh, Blackwater
Vice Admiral Herbert William Sumner Gibson had inherited Hurstleigh from his widowed mother, Louisanna, who was the eldest daughter of the Rt Rev Charles Sumner, Bishop of Winchester (1827-1869). Hurstleigh had been valued for probate at £4,000 after Louisanna's death in 1900. The 1910 tax assessors valued the whole estate at £3,814, including the buildings at £2,451. In 1911, Hurstleigh had twenty-one rooms.

Admiral Gibson was the first cousin of Mrs Alice Louisa Stooks, the wife of Charles Drummond Stooks, Vicar of Yateley (1885-1905) and author of the *History of Crondall and Yateley*.

Yateley Hall
The owners of three of Yateley's houses stated in the census that they had twenty rooms: one was Yateley Manor; the other two were Yateley Lodge and Yateley Hall. All three still stand today. It is immediately apparent that Yateley Hall is somewhat larger than the other two, and larger than Hurstleigh as it is shown in old photographs. Yateley Hall was enlarged after the Second World War, but even so it seems that whoever completed Yateley Hall's census return read the instructions incorrectly. The 1910 tax assessment states that Yateley Hall then had twenty bedrooms, not just twenty rooms.

Yateley Hall, taken from below its ha-ha (sunken stone wall and ditch) from the west, was the home of Miss de Winton Corry. Her widowed mother had died in 1910. With medieval origins, the building is now Grade II* listed, principally because of its remodelling by Richard Norman Shaw. (Malcolm Miller)

The full description reads:

'Old Jacobean Mansion with addition (18th Century) and modern stabling – solidly built in brick & slated – 20 Bedrooms, 5 reception rooms; kitchen, laundry. H.K.R. pantry & offices. Stabling for 6 horses, coachhouse, farm buildings, brick cowhouse and piggeries, dutch barn (iron) and several timber & tiled sheds. Area 43a.3r.36p. Entrance Lodge (3 rooms) and 2 Cottages each 4 rooms.'

Using a modern ranking based on numbers of bedrooms, Yateley Hall, with twenty bedrooms, tops Frogmore Park, with sixteen, and Yateley Manor, with thirteen. Yateley Hall's Victorian additions and remodelling by architect Norman Shaw had been done very sensitively, earning it listed status as Grade II*. The 1910 assessors valued the house at £3,808, the same as Hurstleigh, only a little more than the valuations of Yateley Manor and Yateley Lodge, and £200 lower than Byways, a much smaller new house then just completed on Vigo Lane. Byways, the home of Captain Wilfred Blackden, only had eight bedrooms and four reception rooms.

In 1911, Yateley Hall was a household of nineteen females, with not a single person born in Yateley. Miss Margaret Louisa Catherine Harriett Hugh Erskine de Winton Corry, the owner, was baptized in South Bersted, Bognor Regis, on 15 May 1859. Her father leased Yateley Hall from 1871. After her father died in 1885, Miss de Winton Corry purchased the manorial tenancy of the whole estate from the executors of Henry Parker Collett, who had died some thirty years before. However, until the Law of Property Acts in the 1920s, the ultimate owner of Yateley Hall was still the Ecclesiastical Commissioners, the Lords of the Manor.

In 1914, Miss de Winton Corry was not living alone with her many servants in the large house. Before her mother died in 1909, she had become the legal guardian of two daughters of Brigadier General Sir Gordon Guggisberg.

Guggisberg was a major in the Royal Engineers when war was declared, but he quickly rose in rank. After a distinguished career in the First World War, Guggisberg was appointed Governor and Commander-in-Chief of the Gold Coast (now the Republic of Ghana). In 1905, he had married the famous actress Decima Moore, who had made her debut at the age of 17 singing a leading role in the premier of Gilbert & Sullivan's opera *The Gondoliers*. Immediately war was declared, she threw herself into war work by founding the Women's Emergency Corps. By Armistice Day, she was Director General of the British Empire Leave Club in Paris.

Guggisberg had married Miss Moore a year after his messy divorce from his first wife in 1904. His first wife had become pregnant by a clergyman. It appears Guggisberg may not have been blameless either, as their two eldest daughters were made wards of court, and Miss de Winton Corry was appointed as their guardian. Guggisberg was not allowed to see them. Miss de Winton Corry brought them up as if they were her daughters. When she died, the girls inherited Yateley Hall jointly, together with a single blood relation of Miss Corry's mother. In 1914, Nancy was 15 and Ena was 14. Their wartime scrapbook, purchased on eBay by the

Nancy and Ena Guggisberg were wards of court, Miss de Winton Corry being their guardian. She treated them as if they were her daughters. This image gives a glimpse of what it was like to grow up in privileged society before the Great War. (Richard Johnston)

Society's Archivist, gives us an insight into the lives of privileged teenagers during the war.

Before the First World War, the class system was still entrenched in the village. The gentry, such as Miss de Winton Corry, lived in the mansions and larger houses. The middle classes were the trades people and artisans, and the working classes were the servants and labourers. Dougie Gibbs, the schoolmaster's son born in the 1920s, tells us that Miss de Winton Corry was always the last to take her pew in church, and the Vicar could not start until she took her seat. If Dougie met a horserider and could not see his face, he always touched his cap because the rider was probably gentry. The gentry had their own rules, such as presenting calling cards and correctly addressing each other. Military ranks were easy, but the rules also applied to addressing spinster ladies.

Miss de Winton Corry would be mortified to be addressed simply as 'Margaret' – as is the mode in modern books. It was usual then to address the eldest daughter by just her surname and any younger sisters by their first name and surname. For instance, Miss Jubb, the eldest daughter of the family living at Glaston Hill House in Eversley, was Commandant of the local volunteer detachment of the Red Cross (VAD). Her sisters, Miss Emily and Miss Alice, were also VADs during the war serving in the local hospitals.

Yateley Lodge

Although it only had nine bedrooms in the 1910 tax assessors record, Yateley Lodge was sold to Mrs Constance C. Wood in 1908 for £4,400. The assessment states that the house had six bedrooms plus three servants' bedrooms, electric light and the plant to generate it. Mrs Wood (1852-1916) was a daughter of Francis Jervoise Ellis-Jervoise JP DL and Mary Louisa Marx. The Jervoise family had lived at Herriard, just south of Basingstoke, since the

This picture of Yateley Lodge shows its magnificent cedar tree, still growing today in the grounds of this Grade II listed building. At the outbreak of war the house was owned by Mrs Constance Wood, daughter of Francis Jervoise Ellis-Jervoise JP DL of Herriard. After she died in 1916, Yateley Military Hospital was transferred here from the Vicarage. (Jean McIlwaine)

reign of Queen Elizabeth I. In 1885, Constance had married Arthur Hardy Wood, the son of John Wood, a rich industrialist who owned Thedden Grange, on the outskirts of Alton. Her second husband survived her, but seems never to have lived at Yateley Lodge. Her first husband, George Francis Marx, died after only six years of marriage. It was her unmarried eldest daughter by her first marriage, Constance Margaret Marx, who will be a major player in our story of *Yateley in the Great War*. She was 35 when war broke out.

Mrs Wood was obviously ailing by 1911: there was a 'Sick Nurse' from the Royal Berkshire Hospital listed in her household on census day. We know the precise date of her death in March 1916 from an entry in the share register of the Great Western Railway. Her shares, worth £23,401, were transferred to her executors, her two brothers. Francis Henry Tristram Jervoise lived at Herriard Park, a forty-room house and the ancestral seat of the Jervoise family; Arthur Tristram Ellis Jervoise lived at Herriard Grange, a fifteen-room house in the same village.

Hilfield

There has been habitation on the Hilfield site from time immemorial. The ancient field system assarted (enclosed) from Yateley Common is medieval. Documentation proves that a substantial house existed on the copyholding from Elizabethan times. The 1665 Hearth Tax records a house having thirteen hearths, second only to the Manor House, which had fourteen.

The house standing in 1914 had been newly built after a disastrous fire in 1905. The 1910 tax assessors described the house as a 'brick & tiled Mansion in good repair – well built with 11 Bedrooms'. Its size, modern construction and amenities probably gave the building itself the highest valuation in Yateley – £8,698, more than double that of the Manor House.

John Packenham Stilwell had been the owner of Hilfield since the death in 1871 of his father-in-law, William Stevens. In 1849, the latter had purchased the copyholding from Captain Henry Browne Mason, the brother of Captain George Mason, who had started the Yateley Volunteers and owned the Manor House.

Hilfield was the home of John Packenham Stilwell, Navy Agent and owner of the eponymous bank in Pall Mall. All three sons who grew up here reached the rank of colonel in the Territorial Forces. His youngest daughter, Beatrice Stilwell, became Quartermaster of the local Red Cross detachment, working herself to an early death. Hilfield was demolished after the Second World War. (Jean McIlwaine)

J.P. Stilwell was the principal owner of the bank called Stilwell & Sons, whose office was then at 42 Pall Mall, Westminster. As well as being a banker, he was one of only four Navy Agents in the country. A Navy Agent was a banker and attorney who was appointed and registered for each ship in the Royal Navy in order to distribute prize money, salvage money, proceeds from capturing slave ships etc. The Navy Agent received 2½ per cent of all moneys so distributed; the commanding officer received 10 per cent of the prize money and then each officer, petty officer and rating down to the ship's boy would each get shares. Midshipmen and chief petty officers received twelve shares each, able seaman four shares and boys one share. Prize money was still distributed to Royal Navy ships during the Great War.

Stilwell (1832-1921) had retired from his bank in 1909, leaving his three sons as the managing partners. He and his wife, Georgina

Elizabeth née Stevens (1842-1916), had seven children. All except the eldest daughter, Norah, who was probably looking after her ageing parents, will play significant roles in our story.

Of the four daughters, Beatrice Ellen Stilwell (1876-1928) had already taken up a prominent position in the British Red Cross. When in 1909 the ladies of Yateley and Eversley had formed the local Voluntary Aid Detachment, Hants 94, she had been appointed Quartermaster. Two of her elder sisters were also VADs.

J.P. Stilwell's grandson, Jack, was the son of Geoffrey Holt Stilwell (1865-1927), known to his family as Holt. He is best known to Yateley people as the author of the *History of Yateley*, edited by Sydney Loader. Jack recalled in a memoir the circumstances in 1914:

'[His father] *and his two brothers, Bernard and Billy were the partners when war broke out in 1914, their father having retired* [from the Stilwell Bank] *some years previously. The brothers were called up at once, and Holt was offered a Brigade if he could re-join, but having retired from the regiment in 1913 he felt it was his duty to continue serving at the bank until his brothers returned after the war.'*

A photograph from the Stilwell family album. (Jean McIlwaine)

F Company of the 4th Battalion Hampshire Regiment trained at the Drill Hall, Yateley, and was officered by members of the Stilwell family of Hilfield. This picture shows the church parade in 1911, with the White Lion and Post Office in the background. (Jean McIlwaine)

The two younger Stilwell brothers were immediately called up because they were both serving officers in the Territorial Army in the 4th Battalion of the Hampshire Regiment, F Company being based at the Drill Hall in Yateley. Geoffrey Holt Stilwell had retired from the Territorial Army as a lieutenant colonel, the rank which both of his younger brothers would attain during the war.

CHAPTER 1

1914

4th Battalion Hampshire Regiment

Some months after war was declared, Major Bernard Stilwell found himself second-in-command of the 2/4th Battalion Hampshire Regiment in Quetta, India, near the present-day Pakistan-Afghan border. In a contribution to *Tiger*, the battalion magazine, he recalled the mobilization of the Yateley company of the 4th Battalion the day after war was declared:

> '*We were a cyclist battalion, and it was the 5th August, 1914. We were all peacefully following our several occupations when at mid-day a bolt from the blue, in the shape of a telegram descended on each of us, and in peremptory words ordered us then and there to report to Headquarters. Thereupon we all dashed home, jumped into uniform, stuffed a toothbrush and a piece of soap in our haversacks, and rushed down to the station to catch the train. In the case of the writer a most impressive send off from the house of his ancestors amid waving of hankerchiefs of the local inhabitants who had turned out in force, was much spoiled by a well-meaning but cow-hocked parlourmaid who came sprinting down the road in pursuit with an umbrella which she thought should be taken to war. Having caught our train we each spent the journey in making out lists of necessaries and unnecessaries we had forgotten to pack; and writing out long telegrams requesting the immediate despatch of the most vital articles on the list.*'

Monday 3 August 1914, the normal summer bank holiday, had been extended by the government until Thursday the 6th because of the emergency. Major Stilwell's jokey style masks the fact that the mobilization of the 4th Hants cannot have been a great surprise to him, or to any other officers in the Territorial Army. On 5 August, the *Daily Telegraph* recorded on page 7:

> *'A Royal Proclamation under the King's own hand was read out by Mr Asquith in the House of Commons yesterday calling out the Army Reserve and embodying the Territorials. These operations have already begun, and a call to arms is meeting with a rapid and enthusiastic response.'*

It is also significant that Bernard Stilwell left for war from Hilfield, his parents' house in Yateley. He then lived at Townfield in Dorking, where he had been born in 1873. He had not been living at his ancestral home since he married Maude Currie at St Peter's Church; 5 August 1914 was their ninth wedding anniversary. He and his younger brother, William Byron Stilwell, who lived in Fleet, were the two senior officers of F Company, 4th Hants. They probably wanted to be close to Yateley Drill Hall when war was declared, expecting to have to march their men out of Yateley to man a strategic position to defend England from invasion. Instead, they had to travel to Winchester to be briefed that they should muster their companies on Salisbury Plain.

Despite the training they received, the War Office still considered these Territorials as amateurs unfit for front-line duty. Because Regular regiments were still largely dispersed throughout the Empire in 1914, the War Office decided to bring back the Regulars to fight on the front line in France, and to replace them in the garrisons abroad with the new territorial regiments. These 'part-time' soldiers had not signed up for service abroad, but to defend Britain. They did not come directly under the control of the War Office, but reported to the Lord Lieutenant of the County – harking right back to the Elizabethan Musters. Territorial officers and men were therefore given the option as to

Lieutenant Colonel J.B.L. (Bernard) Stilwell (of Yateley) is leading the 2/4th half battalion, Hampshire Regiment, to the brigade training camp at Kolpur, the highest point of the Bolan Pass in Baluchistan (now in Pakistan), and the last town on the railway before Quetta. The 2/4ths had been sending drafts of fresh men to reinforce the 1/4th Hants fighting their way up the Tigris to Baghdad. This photograph was taken in September 1916, seven months before the 2/4ths were transferred to Suez in Egypt for combat service. Many Yateley men were serving in both half battalions. (Christopher Bunch)

whether they wanted to serve abroad. Most Yateley men signed up. The 4th Hants was split into two half regiments at Bustard Camp, being strengthened with new recruits. Each half regiment was commanded by a Regular officer, with the two younger Stilwell brothers as seconds-in-command: Major W.B. Stilwell in the 1/4ths and Major J.B.L. Stilwell in the 2/4ths.

A short article dated 25 September 1914 in *Ringing World*, the weekly journal for church bell ringers, gives us a glimpse of an enjoyable break for some of our local men from the rigorous military training at Bustard Camp on Salisbury Plain. They had heard that a 'nice ring of six bells' was available at Amesbury. A group, which included Lance-Corporal Cyril Bunch and brothers Privates George and Charles Butler, walked the 7 miles, arriving about 4.00 pm at the church. They returned to camp by curfew at 9.30 pm after 'enjoying a very nice Sunday afternoon' bellringing. Charles Butler would be killed in Belgium on 14 April 1918.

Cyril Bunch had his twentieth birthday on 1 February earlier that year. Charles Butler was even younger: his eighteenth birthday had been on 3 July. His brother, George, would be 22 on 22 October. They were sons of George Edward William Butler, the farm bailiff for Captain Richard Geaves of Yateley Manor. There was an older brother, William, who was also training with them in the 4th Hants at Bustard Camp. Elizabeth Butler was one of several Yateley mothers who had three or more sons on active service. The family lived at Manor Lodge, later called Manor Cottage, opposite the Plough Inn. They therefore lived across the main road from the business premises and home of Cyril Bunch's father, Mr J.R. Bunch, described in Kelly's 1915 edition as a builder.

The Bunches and Butlers were just the sort of men who had been the backbone of the Rifle Volunteer movement since it had been formed in 1859 against a perceived threat of invasion from Napoleon III's France. The artisans, tradesmen and shopkeepers of Yateley and its surrounding district had trained each week and attended summer camps each year. They had built a rifle range on Yateley Common, with its 900-yard firing position, just south of the Anchor Inn on Vigo Lane, the butts being way over near the present go-kart track. Captain George Mason, a Peninsular War veteran, had willingly reduced his rank to lieutenant to command the Yateley Rifle Volunteers. Colonel Sir Thomas Sturmy Cave, who commanded the 1st Volunteer Battalion when it was renamed the 4th Battalion Hampshire Regiment in 1909, was the son of the owner of the brewery in Hartley Wintney. He had joined Yateley Rifle Volunteers when he was 18. Several Yateley Volunteers had served in the Boer War. At the outbreak of war, F Company was made up of about 100 men drawn from Yateley and the surrounding villages – just the right sort of men to replace the Regular soldiers defending the Empire.

As ex-public schoolboys the three sons of John Pakenham Stilwell of Hilfield had immediately gained commissions in the Volunteers. In 1894, the Stilwell family had provided the land for the Drill Hall and a small-bore rifle range behind it in 1909.

The first page of the bank account of the Yateley company of the 4th Battalion of the Hampshire Regiment. Warren's Winchester Directory 1914 records Colonel Sir T. Sturmy Cave KCB of Kilmont Woking, Surrey, as the Honorary Colonel of the battalion, commanded by Lieutenant Colonel G.H. Stilwell of Windlesham, Surrey. The 4th Hants had eight companies, with depots at Winchester, Alton, Aldershot, Andover, Basingstoke and Yateley. (Yateley Society Archive)

These new facilities appear on the 1910 OS maps, but not on the 1894 revision. On the other hand, the 900-yard range on the common appears on the 1871 and 1894 editions but not on the 1910 one. Training in rifle marksmanship in the Yateley company was obviously good. In the 1930s, Cyril Bunch would shoot for England in international competitions at Bisley.

Unfortunately there are no existing copies of the *Yateley Parish Magazine* as they were destroyed when St Peter's Church was burnt down in 1979 to conceal the theft of its Victorian musical instruments. Copies of the *Eversley Parish Magazine* during the First World War do exist. The Rector of Eversley, the Rev H. Mosley, in a long article dated 28 September 1914, first commented about the harvest thanksgiving services:

F Company, 4th Hants, at Bustard Camp on Salisbury Plain in autumn 1914. The card was sent by Private George Cranham (4/2967) of Blackwater to his mother, telling her to remember to put his Service number on her letters and address them c/o Embarkation Office, Southampton. He remarked that 'we shan't be sorry to be moving for it's jolly cold at nights now'. (Yvonne Allen)

> *'It was interesting to see a sprinkling of khaki in the morning in the uniforms of some of our young men who have recently joined the Territorial forces, or were already members, and who had received 48 hours leave before rejoining their camp prior to sailing for India at the end of this week. It was inspiring to join in the well-known hymns and in the singing at both services of the National Anthem, although at this time our minds are inevitably somewhat pre-occupied with thoughts that do not altogether partake of the festal.'*

The 1/4th sailed for India on 9 October 1914 and landed at Karachi on 11 November that year. The 2/4th sailed for India on 13 December 1914 on the SS *Caledonia*, arriving at Karachi on 11 January 1915. The 2/4th were posted to Quetta (now Quetta Staff College of the Pakistan Army) for two years. This half battalion constantly exchanged men with the 1/4th, who were to become heavily engaged in fighting the Turkish Army in Mesopotamia (modern-day Iraq).

Auxiliary Military Hospitals
In the same article that he announced the imminent departure of the local Territorials to India, the Rector of Eversley gave full details about the setting up of the Yateley Auxiliary Military Hospital.

Yateley Vicarage.

T.H.
B.

Yateley's Vicarage in the First World War is now a listed building called Glebe House. Until Rev Harry Sumner was installed as Vicar at St Peter's in 1874, Yateley's previous incumbents had been perpetual curates and therefore tended to have private means. Rev Robert Clarke Caswall established the Vicarage on Vicarage Lane at his own expense, and the Rev Charles Drummond Stooks extended it. (Malcolm Miller)

There were to be two wards, one at Yateley Vicarage and the other at Firgrove just over the parish boundary in Eversley:

> *'Announcement was made at both services yesterday as to a spirited and patriotic enterprise by Miss Tindal in opening a private Hospital at Fir Grove for wounded or convalescent soldiers from the front. This is more strictly a ward of the hospital started at Yateley, and is to be known as the Fir Grove Ward. Miss Tindal's effort arose from a Red Cross meeting held at Yateley early in August, at which the Vicar of Yateley came forward with an offer of the Vicarage to the Red Cross Society for providing about 20 beds for convalescants. This offer Miss Tindal expressed her wish to supplement with 10 beds at Fir Grove, and the pay of a fully trained nurse for an unlimited time, as well as the kitchen and laundry work. Upon this a pause ensued, due to a rumour that got about to the effect that the Government was not going to avail itself,*

at all events for a long time, of offers of Homes and Hospitals under the Red Cross Society.

'Suddenly, some twelve days ago, the Surgeon-General from Aldershot arrived to inspect the rooms at Fir Grove, and after various enquiries passed them. This was succeeded a few days later by the request that the rooms should be ready by Monday, 28th, this necessitating much hurried preparation and considerable outlay. The War Office allowance towards the expenses of the hospital is 2/- a day per man. Although the War Office has thus undertaken to meet a certain portion of the cost of food and other supplies, and the Red Cross Society is also assisting with some of the surgical requirements, still very considerable additional expense must be connected with the carrying on of the Ward from week to week. The feeding alone of the patients will entail rather a severe strain upon garden and dairy produce, so that contributions of fruit, vegetables and eggs from well-wishers in the village will be most acceptable. In addition to this Miss Tindal suggests other things that might be welcome, such as butter, cakes, pots of jam, buns, potatoes, tobacco, good razors and scented soap, which is thought a great treat.

'Help in the laundry work would also be much valued, so that on washing day Miss Tindal might be sure of one helper at Fir Grove, and on two other days perhaps two others might proffer their services to help the laundry maid with ironing, etc., two to four hours work, meals provided. Doubtless if, as Miss Tindal hopes, offers to help in these various ways, or to provide these various things, should be willingly made, it might be necessary in some way to systematize them, so as both to prevent overlapping and to secure regularity; and that would follow as the willingness to help in these ways is ascertained. But doubtless in any case the need in these matters would begin as soon as the patients for the Hospital arrive. Mr Hills, butcher [in Yateley, with a branch in Eversley], *is being most generous.*

'Let me conclude this summary of what Miss Tindal wishes to place before us with a sentence quoted more closely from her

This photograph is particularly interesting as it shows all the staff necessary for running the military hospital at Firgrove. Miss Tindal, owner of the house and commandant of the hospital, is seated at the centre of the front row. (George Trevis)

letter, in which she says that though she counts it "but a small thing to have only ten men at a time to help back to health and strength, when we think of the thousands who have laid down their lives, still it is something, and she hopes that many tens may pass through our hands and live to bless the day when they had the restorative peace and quiet of an English village – a contrast to the stormy times they have been through, the pain of sleeplessness and hunger, the hardships of heat and cold." I ought to add to this that the Authorities have promised Miss Tindal that the patients sent to the Fir Grove Ward shall, as far as possible, be natives of the counties of Hampshire and Berkshire.'

Miss Anne Tindal was the eldest daughter of Charles Grant Tindal, who had only recently died in January 1914. He had made his money by establishing the first meat canning factory in Australia in 1866, simultaneously taking a licence to produce concentrated beef essence known as 'Liebig's Extract'. Anne Grant Tindal's younger sister, Elizabeth Grant Tindal, had married Geoffrey Holt Stilwell, who, as senior partner of Stilwell & Sons, had elected to continue as a Navy Agent and keep the family-owned bank functioning during the war. Mrs Betty Stilwell's two brothers-in-law, Bernard and Billy, were thus the two aforementioned majors serving in the 4th Hants, about to sail for India.

The sister of Miss Tindal's brothers-in-law was Miss Beatrice Stilwell, Quartermaster of the Red Cross detachment running the two wards of Yateley Auxiliary Military Hospital. In his article on 28 September 1914, the Rector of Eversley also named the Acting Commandant of the local detachment as Miss Marx. She was the eldest daughter of Mrs Constance Wood, the owner of Yateley Lodge.

When Beatrice Stilwell died prematurely in 1928 at the age of 52, her elder sister, Nora, and her many friends wrote and published a book in her memory. Miss Margaret Marx wrote:

'At a meeting at Glaston Hill early in 1909 the decision was taken to form a Voluntary Aid Detachment under the British Red Cross Scheme. The Women's Detachment was known as VAD Hants 94. From the first Beatrice Stilwell was interested and accepted the office of Quartermaster of Hants 94. This entailed studying many forms and understanding a scheme which from its nature was largely tentative. She was provided with a register and set to work to collect in the villages of Yateley and Eversley, promises from everybody of what they would contribute towards a hospital which might be required in the event of war. It is difficult now to understand what that meant as she had in all seriousness to prepare for an event which, in their hearts, no one thought could happen to England.

'From time to time the Register had to be revised, and the efficient way in which this was done was shown in the first week of August 1914, when at a meeting in the Drill Hall at Yateley, the Vicar and his wife, the late Rev J. and Mrs Beardall, offered the Vicarage for a hospital and the Quartermaster *announced that when the Army Medical Authorities accepted the offer of Hants 94 to provide an equipped hospital, she would require the materialisation of the promises. For the interest of those who may have forgotten or never known the scope of her work I may say that those promises ranged from beds and bedding, chairs and tables, spoons and forks, money, groceries and jams to garden produce, and actually included all the innumerable requirements of a household of some 20 people with the comforts so necessary for weary, wounded men. I must remind you that we were undertaking something which had never been done before.*

'The hospital was accepted and was made up to the required number of beds by the generous offer of part of her house by the late Miss Tindal of Fir Grove, Eversley. The first patients arrived on, I believe, October 2nd, 1914.'

After the war was over, the Hampshire Red Cross published its report, giving details of its organization, each VAD unit and its costs and performance. The Vice-President of the Hartley Wintney Division was the Hon. Mrs Anstruther-Gough-Calthorpe of Elvetham Hall, Winchfield, and the Assistant County Secretary was Dr Balgarnie OBE of the Dutch House, Hartley Wintney. The Divisional Hon. Secretary was Miss Jubb of Glaston Hill, Eversley, who was also Commandant of Hants 94.

Dr Wilfred Balgarnie was also the resident doctor at the Minley Auxiliary Military Hospital, which, being only a few hundred yards south of Yateley's parish boundary, was partly staffed by Yateley ladies. Minley was opened on 21 September 1914 with thirty-six beds, increased to seventy-two by the end of the war, taking patients from the Connaught and Cambridge Hospitals in Aldershot. Minley Hospital was somewhat different from other Red Cross hospitals in that it had an operating theatre. Dr Balgarnie had begun the war at Tylney Hall, where his wife was Commandant. Over 100 operations were carried out. Tylney Hall hospital closed on 31 October 1915 and the theatre was transferred to Minley. Minley Hospital operated in a large house called Minley Lodge,

A group of nurses and patients pictured outside Minley Military Hospital. One of the VADs is Miss Evie Geaves. The Geaves family owned Yateley Manor but had moved out during the Great War. Two of the sisters spent most of the war working at this hospital. (Jean McIlwaine)

which was owned by Lawrence Currie of Minley Manor. He was another prominent London banker, being managing partner of Glyn, Mills, Currie & Co, then one of the leading private clearing banks. The Red Cross report states that Mrs Sybil Currie was the Commandant and met all expenses except capitation, which was met by Sir L. Phillips, Bart. However, an accompanying table showing costs states that the grant from the Army for the whole war was £10,229 9s 2d, with donations amounting to £2,628 8s 6d. This last sum is almost the same of the total donations to the Yateley and Firgrove Hospitals combined, but the Army grant to Yateley Hospital was under £7,500.

The house in which the Minley Hospital was established had, until the previous year, been the residence of Sir Arthur Godley. Sir Arthur had been created the first Lord Kilbracken in 1909, the year he had retired as Permanant Under-Secretary of State for India, the most senior Civil Servant in the India Office. Lord Kilbracken's eldest daughter was the Hon. Mrs Katherine Euphemia Coleridge, married to John Duke Coleridge, the architect.

Minley Lodge had been the home of Sir Arthur Godley, created the 1st Lord Kilbracken in 1909. He had been Permanent Under-Secretary of State at the India Office for twenty-six years. The house was part of the Minley Estate owned by the Currie family, prominent London bankers. At the outbreak of war, the house being vacant, Mrs Sybil Currie offered it as a Red Cross hospital and became its commandant. Dr Wilfred Balgarnie of Hartley Wintney ran its operating theatre. The house was demolished in the Second World War. (Jean McIlwaine)

Belgian Refugees

John Duke Coleridge had purchased some land in Darby Green in 1908 where he built a house to his own design. He and his wife did not move in until after the 1911 census, as they were then living at 54 Oxford Terrace, Edware Road. Darby Green House, sited on what we now call Stroud Lane, was a seven-bedroom building valued with its grounds for Land Tax at £2,247.

It was the execution of the German army's so-called Schlieffen Plan which brought Great Britain into the Great War. Germany's intended lightning strike on Paris entailed outflanking the French army, in the process violating Belgian neutrality. The Belgian government had refused the German army peaceable transit. The atrocities in eastern Belgium forced a wave of Belgian refugees westward before the advance of the German army and, when there was effectively nowhere else to go, at least a quarter of a million Belgians arrived at British ports, principally Folkestone.

This was the largest influx of refugees in British history. In a rush of sympathy, local organizations were set up to deal with this unprecedented crisis. Mrs Matilda Shakspeare, the wife of the County Councillor, set up the Yateley Committee to support the Basingstoke branch of the Belgian Refugee Fund. Empty houses were found to house refugee families, and places at school were found for their children.

We know about one refugee family from Sydney Loader, one of the two founding Vice-Presidents of the Yateley Society. In a short but intriguing paragraph in Sydney's unpublished memoirs, *The Changing Scene*, he wrote:

> '*During the first war Darby Green House was let to the Count de Borchgrave and his family. They also had Heathcroft for a time. He was a Belgian refugee. His wife was very pleasant but he was difficult. They had three sons and all the family rode bicycles. There was also a housebike, a funny old thing hard to manage as the front brake, the only one, came down on top of the front tyre, which could easily put you over the handlebars.*'

Sydney was 9 years old when war broke out. He spent his childhood living in the unlisted half-timbered thatched cottage now known as Old Cottage in the Darby Green Conservation Area. The customary name for this property is Heathcroft, and a cottage of that name can be securely traced back in the manorial court books to before 1700. Before the First World War, James Loader, Sydney's father, worked as gardener for Captain John Masterman, who owned a big new house built in the grounds of the Old Cottage. Confusingly, the customary name Heathcroft was transferred to the new grand house, and the old cottage had no name until it just became known as the Old Cottage.

Count Adrien de Borchgrave d'Altena first lived at Darby Green House, the Coleridges' new house. John Duke Coleridge was living in Paddington, as he joined the Royal Navy in December 1914, serving as an Able Seaman in an anti-aircraft battery formed to protect London from raids by Zeppelin airships. By the following

Heathcroft·   may 4 1930

Heathcroft, now demolished, was built in the 1880s. From 1902 it was the home of Captain John Masterman RN. After his death in 1915, his widow leased it to the Count de Borchgrave, who was already leasing Darby Green House next door. After the count and his family moved to West London, Mrs Masterman moved back into Heathcroft. After the war, the house was sold to Admiral J.R.P. Hawksley, who lived there until his death in 1955. (the late Sydney Loader)

June he had been given a commission and spent the rest of the war based at Scapa Flow in the Orkneys. It is probable that his wife spent the early part of the war at their London home, as the birth of their third child, Arthur Nicholas, was registered in Paddington in November 1915.

Mrs Shakspeare was consistently able to raise very high donations from Yateley people for the Belgian Refugee Relief Fund.

The *Hants & Berks Gazette* of 10 October 1914 states that the Harvest Festival collection at St Peter's raised £23. This is equivalent to about £2,400 in today's money, reflecting the relative affluence of the Yateley families living in their big houses compared with a farming village of similar size. The count was paid £4 per week by the Relief Fund, but Ernest Debeffe, the head of another Belgian refugee family in Yateley, was paid only about 15s (75p) per month. Suzanne Debeffe (b. 27 August 1906) attended the Yateley village school in 1914.

On Friday 3 March 1916, the personal columns of *The Times* contained a sad notice: the death at Winton Cottage, Yateley, of Daniel Frank Dieltiens, aged only 18 days. His grave can still be seen in the children's corner of St Peter's churchyard, recording that he was born on 10 Feb and died on the 28th, the son of F. and D. Dieltiens. It is only such poignant evidence which continues to remind us of the presence of Belgian refugees living in Yateley. No references to Yateley have yet been found on the official Refugee registration cards.

Sydney Loader stated that the Belgian count 'also had Heathcroft for a time'. Captain John Masterman died at Heathcroft in July 1915. Neither of Masterman's two sons was at home, so it is possible that Mrs Masterman moved out for a period to allow the count to occupy both Darby Green House and Heathcroft, which were next-door to each other. It appears that the count and his family did not remain long in Yateley, as his wife had two more babies, a son born in Fulham in January 1917 and a daughter born in Twickenham in March 1919.

The Impact of the War on the Community

Yateley differed from other towns and villages at the outbreak of the war. It was obviously different from the northern towns and cities which enthusiastically raised Pals Battalions, contributing large numbers to Kitchener's New Armies. Yateley also differed from nearby villages such as Hartley Wintney.

This can in part be seen from the Roll of Honour published on 19 December 1914 by the *Hants & Berks Gazette* in an attempt to list all the men in their area of coverage who would be away from home at Christmas. A comparison of Hartley Wintney Yateley reveals major differences. In the Hartley Wintney list, twelve men were serving in 'Kitchener's Army', whereas none were so listed for Yateley. There were far fewer Regulars in Hartley Wintney, even though its population was 15 per cent larger.

Of the fifty-seven men listed from Yateley, about 40 per cent of them were serving in the 4th Battalion of the Hampshire Regiment. Another third (nineteen) were already serving as Regulars in the army, not surprising when considering Yateley's proximity to Aldershot. More surprisingly, eleven men were serving in the Royal Navy, some of these recently called back as Reservists. In total, therefore, about half of the Yateley men in this Roll of Honour already mobilized in December 1914 were Regulars or Reservists, and the other half had already trained as Territorials.

By the end of the war, a quarter of the entire male population of Britain had joined up, but half of those had to be conscripted from the start of 1916. The total male population of Yateley in 1921 was 915, which suggests that about 230 might have served during the war. In fact the number was far higher, due to the average age of the male population and the rapid turnover of the entire Yateley population.

Approximately 350 Yateley men listed in the 1911 census became eligible for military service during the war. Of these, about 290 were between the ages of 18 and 41 in August 1914. The *Hants & Berks* Roll of Honour suggests about 20 per cent of the eligible male population of Yateley was serving in the forces by Christmas 1914. It also suggests that there was no big recruiting rush in Yateley, because a fifth of Yateley manhood had reported for duty on 5 August, if they were not already serving somewhere around the world.

Many First World War service papers were subsequently destroyed, some by enemy bombing during the Second World War. Despite this lack of service records, our research has identified 102 men with strong Yateley connections who had joined up by Christmas 1914. As only fifty-seven Yateley men were listed in the

Hants & Berks Gazette as serving by Christmas 1914, it seems that many Yateley men were not included.

The Hartley Wintney list contains a total of ninety names, many more than Yateley, even though its population was not much higher. This suggests that sales of the Basingstoke newspaper to Yateley households were lower than in Hartley Wintney, accounting for the missing Yateley names. On the other hand, the total numbers in both villages may well be artificially high because parents had sent in names of sons not actually resident in either village.

It has already been noted that the two Stilwell brothers, officers of the 4th Hants, did not then live in Yateley, even though they were born and brought up in the village. Likewise, Mrs Jessie Doris Brown, the widow of Colonel F.D.M. Brown VC, put forward the names of her four sons and stepsons to the *Hants & Berks Gazette*,though none lived in Yateley. Two were Gurkha officers, one was a Royal Marine officer and her youngest son, Reginald Llewellyn Brown, was still a Cadet in the Royal Engineers at Woolwich. The latter was known as Llewyn to his family and friends, but in later life was also known as Bruno professionally.

Strictly speaking, Llewellyn Brown was not on active service in December 1914 because he had already been interned at Ruhleben in Germany, where John Cecil Masterman, the younger son of Captain John Masterman of Heathcroft, had also been interned. Both these man went on to have illustrious careers. Sir John Masterman, Vice Chancellor of Oxford University 1957-1958, chaired the famous MI5 XX committee during the Second World War, which among other exploits, by deception, tied down German forces in the Pas-de-Calais not only before but well after D-Day in 1944. Major General Reginald Llewellyn Brown became Director-General of the Ordnance Survey. He had married the daughter of John Duke Coleridge and Katherine Euphemia née Godley of Darby Green House. The Yateley Society honoured him as one of our two founder vice-presidents.

If some names could be subtracted from the 1914 Roll of Honour were it restricted to men actually resident in Yateley, then

YATELEY.

'I hope you will get this in time for Christmas and this card will remind you of many happy warm hearted occasions and hope that many more are in store for you. As you can't be at home I hope you will have a pleasant occupation and see something beautiful. Love from J' [card marked 'Gen L Brown'] Llewellyn Brown was interned at Ruhleben in 1914. He had been enjoying a walking holiday in the Harz Mountains at the outbreak of war. (Jean McIlwaine)

other residents should be added. William Burroughs Tice, who ran the bakery at Goose Green Cottage on Yateley Green, had three sons who served in the Great War. Harold Ernest Tice is listed by the *Hants & Berks Gazette* as a Territorial serving in the Surrey Yeomanry. He would reach the rank of company quartermaster sergeant in the East Surrey Regiment, amply qualifying him to extend his father's business by taking over Yateley's main store by the church after the war. Inexplicably though, his younger brother, William Henry Tice, is not listed on the Roll of Honour. He had joined the Royal Navy in 1904, serving continuously until he was invalided out in 1916 with heart disease. Obviously a man with a keen sense of duty, he promptly went back to sea in the merchant service.

There were other men already serving in the Royal Navy who were not included in the December 1914 Roll of Honour, notably Royal Marine Gunner Lloyd Charles Wheeler. Together with Able

The signatures on this envelope from a hotel in Baden Baden were collected by Andrew Sheldon's grandmother in October 1914. At the outbreak of war, she was on an extended holiday in Freiburg with her mother and sisters. John Cecil Masterman from Yateley, whose signature appears as J.C. Masterman, was at Freiburg University as an exchange lecturer from Oxford when he was rounded up. There are many other signatures of men later famous, including Sir John Balfour, head of the American Department of the Diplomatic Service in the Second World War, and Sir Timothy Eden Bart. From this hotel the ladies were repatriated, but the men were interned at Ruhleben. (Image and research courtesy of Andrew Sheldon)

Seaman Mark Hammond from Brandy Bottom, he had already lost his life in the Battle of Coronel in the South Atlantic on 1 November when HMS *Good Hope* was sunk. They were the first two Royal Navy men born and brought up in Yateley who were killed in the Great War. Lloyd Wheeler's father, Owen, was described in the admission books of the village school as a hawker of Vigo Lane. When Owen and Jane Wheeler baptized their ten children at St Peter's, the Vicar usually noted the father's occupation as pedlar. Many gypsy families parked their vans and pitched tents on Yateley

Common at Vigo Lane. Lloyd Wheeler was the first of the many gypsy men educated in Yateley village school who gave his life in war service.

About half of Yateley's regular naval personnel were not represented in the *Hants & Berks Gazette*'s Roll of Honour. John Duke Coleridge, already mentioned, was another example, although he had two homes, one in Yateley and the other in Paddington. Inexplicably, only the eldest son of the Butlers of Yateley Manor Lodge appears in the newspaper. The two sons who joined the bellringing trip to Avebury are missing from the list.

By Christmas 1914, a large proportion of men had already left the village, including the younger men who had sailed for India. A large proportion of those had left immediately in August. It was the wives and daughters who had to cope with bringing up their large families, tending their gardens and allotments and in some cases billeting troops, at the same time as working at the military hospitals as nurses, cooks and laundry maids.

Christmas 1914
There are many stories about Christmas 1914. The two teenage girls at Yateley Hall pasted into their scrapbook the letter sent out by Princess Mary to raise funds for her Christmas Box. Princess Mary wanted 'every sailor afloat and every soldier at the front' to have the present. The contents were tailored to the recipients, including the Ghurkas, Sikhs and nurses serving at the front. As the princess raised more than enough to accomplish this, the eligibility was widened and 2,620,019 presents were eventually distributed. The gesture obviously caught the imaginations of the two Misses Guggisberg, who most probably contributed generously.

Life and leadership in the community were changing, not all of it attributable to the war, but as a response to it. J.P. Stilwell, who had taken a leading role in church and parish affairs, was 82. His eldest son, Holt, managing the bank, was living in the family house in London. The other two sons had already left with their regiment for India and the Middle East. Beatrice Stilwell, undoubtedly with formidable organizational skills and a phenomenal work ethic, was running the

BUCKINGHAM PALACE.

October 15th, 1914.

For many weeks we have all been greatly concerned for the welfare of the sailors and soldiers who are so gallantly fighting our battles by sea and land. Our first consideration has been to meet their more pressing needs, and I have delayed making known a wish that has long been in my heart for fear of encroaching on other funds, the claims of which have been more urgent.

I want you all now to help me to send a Christmas present from the whole nation to every sailor afloat and every soldier at the front. On Christmas-eve when, like the shepherds of old, they keep their watch, doubtless their thoughts will turn to home and to the loved ones left behind, and perhaps, too, they will recall the days when as children themselves they were wont to hang out their stockings wondering what the morrow had in store.

I am sure that we should all be the happier to feel that we had helped to send our little token of love and sympathy on Christmas morning, something that would be useful and of permanent value, and the making of which may be the means of providing employment in trades adversely affected by the war. Could there be anything more likely to hearten them in their struggle than a present received straight from home on Christmas-day?

Please, will you help me?

Mary.

Princess Mary wanted to make sure that all troops serving at the front had a Christmas present in 1914, and sent this letter nation-wide asking for help. This copy was pasted into the scrapbook kept by the Guggisberg girls at Yateley Hall. (Richard Johnston)

family estate in addition to her role as Quartermaster of the two wards of the military hospital. Dr John Mills, for years a leading light in the community, had died in April 1913. His son, John Coleridge Mills, an engineering student at London University, was appointed temporary Second Lieutenant on 9 September 1914 and would be killed in

France on 25 September 1915. Dr Mills' daughter, Margaret Sophie Mills, was one of the original team which formed Hants 94 Red Cross Detachment in 1909, becoming Assistant Quartermaster of Yateley Military Hospital. She studied for a medical degree after the war and eventually emigrated to Vancouver, Canada. One of the constants in the village was Miss de Winton Corry at Yateley Hall. She played her part by allowing battalions of Kitchener's Army to camp and train in her grounds, and taking in Belgian refugee families.

Because Yateley had prepared for the possibility of war, three local houses were functioning as hospitals by Christmas 1914, staffed by trained local women, while many of Yateley's younger men were already sailing for India to put into effect the training they had had at summer camps. Yateley Common had long been a training area for Sandhurst cadets. Almost from the outbreak of war, battalions of volunteers from all over the country arrived to train in the parish. They all had to be fed, watered and accommodated.

This group portrait of the seventeen ladies of VAD 94 shows them at summer camp in June 1914. It is an illustration from the 'In Memoriam' book produced by her sister Norah following Beatrice's (BES in the photograph) early death in 1928. Also identified in the photo is Miss Margaret Marx (CMM), who lived at Yateley Lodge with her mother before twice serving overseas as a volunteer nurse. (Yateley Society Archive)

CHAPTER 2

1915

A German Spy in Yateley?

As the New Year opened, an incident widely reported around the country enables us to determine which brigades of which divisions of Kitchener's New Army were billeted and training in Yateley.

The following extract is from the *Western Times* of 1 January 1915:

> *'GERMAN FINED For Seeking to Elicit Military Secrets Relating to Coast Defence*
>
> *'At Aldershot, yesterday, a German named Constantine Von Meien, was fined £10, or in default two months' imprisonment, for having attempted to elicit information from Company Sergeant-Major Nesbitt, of the 11th Northumberland Fusiliers, relating to the defences of the ports between Sunderland and Hull. Sergeant-Major Nesbitt said that while in a hotel in Yateley,* [the] *accused, in conversation, asked* [the] *witness questions regarding East Coast defences.* [The w]*itness informed the officer, and the defendant was arrested.'*

An article in the *Birmingham Mail* on Christmas Eve stated that 'the accused got into conversation with Nesbitt the day after the German raid on the east coast.' In this raid, on 16 December 1914, the German Navy had fired about 1,150 shells at Scarborough, Whitby and West Hartlepool, killing 137 people, mostly civilians, and injuring more than 530. The press and the general public were outraged at the German Navy, and the Royal Navy for failing to

Troops on the green outside the Dog & Partridge. The men are wearing the blue uniform issued to Kitchener's New Armies before standard khaki became available. Note the variety of forage caps being worn. Their rifles appear to be Lee Metfords. The evidence indicates that this postcard was probably produced early in 1915, when battalions of volunteers were being trained on Yateley Common. They were dispatched to France in the autumn, after about twelve months' training. (Malcolm Miller)

defend them. In this context it is not surprising that the Von Meien incident was reported nationwide.

Constanin George Carl von Meien was 64 years old, single and living with his two sisters at a house called Constantia, on the edge of Yateley Green. In 1911, he was living in Yateley 'on his own means', but in the 1891 census his occupation was cotton broker. He died in Staines in 1941, aged 90, so he had again been subject to official scrutiny as an enemy alien in 1939. His card exempting him from internment tells us he was born in Lippe (near Detmold), Germany, on 7 December 1850 and was a retired banker in 1939.

Kitchener's New Armies

Company Sergeant Major Thomas Nesbitt 11/8876 had joined the Northumberland Fusiliers in 1891, aged 19, and had served in India, Egypt and South Africa in the Boer War. Having been transferred to the Army Reserve in 1902, he was called back as a Special Reservist in 1914. The 11th Battalion of the Northumberland Fusiliers was formed at Newcastle in September 1914 and came under orders of 68 Brigade,

23rd Division. This division was established in September 1914 as part of Army Order 388, authorizing Kitchener's Third New Army.

Nesbitt was attested on 9 September 1914 and immediately promoted to sergeant. Eight days later, he was promoted company quartermaster sergeant. He sailed for France with the 11th Northumberland Fusiliers on 25 August 1915, having the rank of company sergeant major. He rose to temporary regimental sergeant major on 2 May 1917, having been mentioned in despatches that January.

It is not surprising that this newly formed battalion chose to do its training in and around Yateley. The second-in-command of the battalion was none other than Major Wilfred Worsley Blackden, who had built his new house, Byways, on Vigo Lane in part of the grounds of Yateley Hall. No doubt he could offer his commanding officer a comfortable bed, whilst his men were boarded out in local houses, school rooms and even barns and tents, enduring the extreme cold of that winter. Major Blackden was then 52, having retired like CSM Nesbitt in 1902, but having served with the Royal Munster Fusiliers in Burma. In October 1914, he re-enlisted to serve with Kitchener's New Armies.

In a small village such as Yateley, Major Blackden was almost certainly well acquainted with Von Meien, who had lived in England for at least forty-five years. His two sisters shown in the 1911 census as living with him in Yateley were recorded in the 1871 census for Islington, living with their widowed mother, a teacher. In the circumstances of the public outrage at the Scarborough raid, Blackden undoubtedly felt obliged to report him to the authorities. It is also not surprising that, not knowing the full story, the *Lincolnshire Echo* thought the £10 fine was derisory.

Major Blackden had lived in Yateley since 1908 and was a governor of Yateley Village School. The school was used as a social centre for the billeted troops. It is good that Major Blackden was able to spend time with his family in Yateley during this period of training: exactly one year later he was dead, having died of wounds in hospital in Étaples on 10 January 1916. He left £40,632 in his will, a not inconsiderable sum in those days.

"Byways", Yateley.

Byways was a new house built just before the First World War for Major Wilfred Worsley Blackden. Born in Quarndon, Derbyshire, he had attended Wellington College before joining the Army. At the outbreak of war he was retired on captain's pay, and was a governor of the village school. He had married Henrietta Anne Grant in Eastbourne in 1896. Major Blackden was killed serving as 2 i/c of a battalion raised in Kitchener's New Armies, but his son, Colin, a lieutenant in the 1st South Wales Borderers, survived. Byways, built in the grounds of Yateley Hall off Vigo Lane, was demolished after the Second World War. (Richard Johnston)

CSM Nesbitt's service record exactly matches that of 68 Brigade, which continued to form part of the 23rd Division. There is further evidence to connect this division to our immediate area. The author, playwright and broadcaster J.B. Priestley was then training with B company of the 10th Battalion of the Duke of Wellington's (West Riding) Regiment. This battalion was part of 69 Brigade, also part of the 23rd Division. Although Priestley does not specifically mention that he trained in Yateley, his letters home provide an excellent insight into the conditions endured by recruits to Kitchener's New Army. On 26 January 1915, his whole battalion started three weeks' intensive training in Eversley. He wrote home:

> '*I am told that Eversley is a very desolate spot and, as the work is very hard, we look like "going through it" … The*

whole battalion has come this time and we are living all over the place. Finchampstead and Cressley are adjoining hamlets, one can barely call them villages for there are houses merely scattered here and there, and only a couple of shops for both places. We are living as we can; some in stables and haylofts, barns, coach houses etc, some in a school, and others, including myself, in empty houses. But we are not all together, as at Camberley, but scattered all over the place. God knows how we are going to get anything to eat! They gave us breakfast this morning in barracks, then we walked the 12 to 14 miles here.'

There is no such place called Cressley. Was Priestley actually referring to Yateley as one of the desolate places, and to Yateley Village School? In Eversley, the Yorkshiremen learned to dig trenches and lay barbed-wire. They left for the barracks in Aldershot on 20 February, and by 1 March 1915 had completed their long march to Shorncliffe Camp, near Folkestone.

The residents of this area may then have had a short respite from troops training, but on 24 April 1915 the *Reading Mercury* reported:

'YATELEY: TROOPS IN THE DISTRICT
'The district has suddenly become an armed camp. On Monday a division marched in. On the green the 64th Brigade R F A are quartered, while in the Park at Yateley Hall a strong force of infantry is quartered. In the distance there is another canvas camp on the Ridges. Manoeuvres are daily taking place.'

It is remarkable that this news item slipped past the DORA (Defence of the Realm Act) censors. 64 Brigade was one of the four field artillery brigades supporting 12th (Eastern) Division, the infantry brigades of which were 35, 36 and 37 Brigades. A division was normally about 12,000-15,000 men. A single brigade of artillery and infantry in two locations suggests Yateley hosted one infantry brigade and its support.

This postcard is from the scrapbook made by the Guggisberg sisters of Yateley Hall. On the back is written 'In the Park in front to the Hall during 1914/18 war'. (Richard Johnston)

This second division to use Yateley for its training moved to France at the end of May. By that time, the Headmaster of Yateley village school was writing in the school logbook: 'May 24 - June 4 Two weeks Whitsun holiday. Extra week as school used for billeting some of 11 Batt. Lancashire Fusiliers.' This battalion formed part of 74 Brigade of 25th Division. This third division to train in Yateley crossed to France at the end of September.

In six months, Yateley people had witnessed three separate divisions of Kitchener's New Army training on the common, on Yateley Green, parading in front of the church, using the school for billeting and refreshments and probably billeted in Yateley with whoever had a spare room. Entries in the school logbook started on 7 December 1914 with, 'Schools used as recreation and refreshment rooms for billeted troops' and continued on 11 December with, 'Heavy rains have seriously affected attendance. Troops make good use of schools daily Sunday included.' This entry was written five days before the shelling of Scarborough. After one more entry on 2 July, 'Minley children have been away on account of roads being blocked by troops', the school logbook falls silent about troops in the village for the rest of the war.

This photograph was included in a book privately published by Miss Norah Stilwell about her dog called Clooty. It shows military tents on Yateley Green during the Great War. (Yateley Society Archive)

There was only one more entry in a local newspaper, the *Reading Mercury* of 4 September 1915:

'SCHOLARS' VISIT TO TRENCHES
'On Wednesday the scholars and teachers of standards V, VI and VII of the Palmer School Wokingham, journeyed to Yateley to see the trenches which have been built on Yateley Flats, similar to those at the front, and also to study the wild flowers etc. Yateley Church was also visited. The bells and wooden tower and the clock were objects of special interest.'

Obviously there were no troops around at the time, and the school trip reads more like a history lesson. Either DORA had successfully stymied any mention of troop movements for the rest of the war or there were none on Yateley Common, or perhaps they became so frequent as no longer to be news. It seems likely that when conscription was introduced in 1916, and new waves of recruits had to be trained, it was a combination of lack of newsworthiness and DORA which has left no contemporary evidence.

There are retrospective memories, and perhaps archaeology to be carried out in the future. Sydney Ireson Loader, who was only 10 in 1915, wrote in his memoirs: 'During the 1914-18 war the soldiers dug a lot of trenches mostly near Cricket Hill, and many of the little hollows in various places were made in the last war as practice slit trenches by the army.'

However, George Ives, who was 21 in 1915, tells us in his memoirs that military training was taking place on Yateley Common even well before the Great War:

'When I was a boy the Common on both sides of the London Road and Flats was used for military training and it used

*to be a regular thing for a regiment of soldiers to camp
in the hollow by the Cricket Hill road. We would often go
up from home for the camp concerts. They were good fun.
Sometimes the whole common would be a camp. There would
be route marches during the summer months from Aldershot
via Hawley up the Flats and back via Minley or vice versa
once or twice a week when two to five thousand soldiers with
bands playing would be marching. During the holidays if we
heard them we would run to see them go by and sometimes
march with the bands. During the 1st World War the common
was used for war training. A replica of the Flanders trenches
was constructed complete with dug-outs and communication
trenches.'*

George Cecil Ives was born on 25 June 1884 in Staplen's Cottage
off the road now called Potley Hill. When he was a boy this was the
main road from Aldershot to Reading. He joined the Royal Navy as
a Boy 2nd Class on 18 April 1911, but was discharged in July 1912.
He re-enlisted in the Royal Naval Air Service on 17 September 1917
as an Air Mechanic Class 1c, giving his trade as carpenter. His next
of kin was his mother, Georgina, of the Cricketers, Yateley – his
parents then ran that pub.

In 1915, George Ives was of an age to take notice and understand
what was going on. He had served in the military but had not yet
re-enlisted. He was the Parish Clerk in the 1950s. His memory of
the military bands must refer to the early years of the century when
he was a boy, rather than to the First World War and the divisions of
Kitchener's Army. His memoir makes it clear that Yateley Common
was not suddenly requisitioned for Great War training, but was just
a continuation of established practice in Aldershot Command.

With all this intensive military activity going on around them,
involving thousands of men, life in the village community carried
on, although it can hardly be described as 'normal'. Because of
the restrictions on reporting, newspapers mostly focussed only on
unfortunate accidents of life, with glimpses of the mundane shown
in the 'small ads'.

This postcard of troops lined up in front of the Dog & Partridge is postmarked 8 February 1915. All except the officers are wearing the 'Kitchener's blue' uniform issued to the New Armies. Many of the men appear to have not yet been issued with a rifle. The rifles already issued had a very long muzzle. (Gordon Harland)

Yateley men volunteer as specialists

Yateley men were continuing to enlist voluntarily, but unlike local men in 1914, and those from all over the country training around them, few of those in 1915 were joining infantry regiments. They were offering their specialist skills as carpenters, mechanics or vehicle drivers. The largest numbers joined the Army Service Corps, Royal Flying Corps and Royal Naval Air Service. Others joined the Artillery, Royal Engineers, Military Police, Remounts and the Medical Corps.

Edwin Bunch was typical of those born and bred in Yateley who, having survived the war, would go on to live in Yateley for the rest of their lives. He was the third son of Daniel and Emily Bunch, who rented a house in Plough Lane from J.P. Stilwell. Emily had ten children, all of whom were baptized at St Peter's, attended the village school and were directly descended from William Bunch, a carpenter who came to Yateley in the early 1700s.

Edwin Bunch was 36 when he stood before the attestation magistrate in Hartley Wintley on 6 March 1915. He stated his

KNELLERS COTTAGES, YATELEY.

In the First World War, the main road we now call the Reading Road was then called Blackwater Road. It then curved north to follow the route of present-day Plough Road, passing the end of what we now call Frys Lane. Even more confusingly, Frys Lane was then called Plough Lane. This area was a hub of activity, with the Plough Inn, Tyler's Stores, two filling stations, J.R. Bunch's builder's yard and a laundry just down Plough Lane. (Richard Johnston)

previous military service had been with the Hampshire Volunteers from 1898-1903, the South African Constabulary and for five years until July 1914 with the 4th Hants. By trade he was a bricklayer, so volunteered for the Royal Engineers. He took to his attestation a letter of recommendation from his employer, James R. Bunch, the builder whose business premises were across the main road from Yateley Manor:

'Dated 27 Feb 1915 at Beech Cottage, Yateley, Hants (telephone Yateley 18)

'Mr Edwin Bunch has been in my employ for the past ten [years]. I have found him to be a most reliable and splendid workman at his trade as bricklayer regular punctual and most energetic

'Signed James R Bunch Builder'

Three weeks later, Edwin Bunch joined the RE at Chatham as a skilled bricklayer, serving in 108th Field Company Royal

Engineers. This unit was attached to the 26th Division, made up mainly of infantry battalions of Kitchener's Third New Army. The division left for France in September 1915 but, because Bulgaria entered the war on the German side on 21 September 1915, it was diverted to Salonika in Greece in November. It remained in that theatre for the rest of the war. Edwin Bunch was tested in December and classed as a 'superior bricklayer'. He was promoted to sergeant in October 1916. On 1 April 1918, he was admitted to 79 Field Ambulance with a fever, and then transferred to 49 General Hospital at Hortiach with malaria. By mid-May he was back with his unit, but in September was granted twenty-one days' leave in the UK, arriving back at his unit in Macedonia on Armistice Day. He was discharged on 13 May 1919.

Of Emily Bunch's ten children, six of her sons and one son-in-law served in the First World War. Her eldest son, Alfred George Bunch, was above the age limit to join up, and her sixth son had a club foot, so did not enlist. William Thomas Bunch, her fifth son, had already emigrated to Australia. He joined up on 26 February 1915 at Beaudesert, Queensland, and served with various units of the Australian Light Horse, mostly in Egypt. He too caught malaria.

The first of Emily's sons to join up was her youngest, Frederick John Bunch. At the age of 18, he had signed up for service abroad with the 4th Hants, together with Cyril Bunch, the bellringer, and Bertram and Jesse, from other branches of the Bunch family. The next of Emily's sons to sign up was her second youngest, Bertie (inscribed as Herbert Bunch on Yateley War Memorial). He had emigrated to Canada in 1911 on the *Albania*, a Cunard liner sailing from Southampton on 2 May. He joined the Canadian Army at Valcartier, Quebec, on 20 September 1914. Like so many other Canadians, Bert Bunch was killed at Ypres on Hill 70 on 15 August 1917.

Samuel Bunch was about two years younger than his brother Edwin. Like all four of Emily's older sons, he had already married by 1914, and was then living at Stoneycroft, Cricket Hill Lane, with his wife, Edith Mary nee Schofield. Like all his brothers, except Walter – who had his own laundry business – Samuel was a bricklayer, probably also working for J.R. Bunch. Samuel had joined the Royal Engineers in 1901 and had bought himself out at Middleburg, South Africa, in 1905. He re-enlisted into the Royal Engineers on 16 November 1914. He joined the 108th Field Company, the same unit which elder brother Edwin would join in March 1915. Samuel therefore served in the British Salonika Force with his brother throughout the rest of the war. He was eventually discharged on 14 May 1919 from Holborn Military Hospital, Mitcham, with a gunshot wound in his right hand, classing him with a 60 per cent disability.

On 28 September 1917, the *London Gazette* published a long list of recipients of military honours: '56886 Sgt S Bunch of Yately' (sic) had been awarded the Military Medal for gallantry. His service papers add that the action was on 8 and 9 May 1917 – the climax of the First Battle of Doiran in Macedonia.

Emily Bunch had two daughters, but the first born, Kate, only lived for four months. Her surviving daughter, Emily May, was 23 when her brother, Edwin, volunteered for the Royal Engineers. She must have been working in Reading, as she married a Reading man, Frederick Peter Chipper, in Reading in 1917. He was not called up until 8 October 1917, when he was 22, and discharged only ten months later. He had served briefly in the Army Veterinary Corps. Since he was awarded the Silver War Badge, Freddy Chipper must have been injured on duty.

Walter Bunch was the eldest of Emily's sons to enlist. He had registered under the so-called Derby Scheme on 12 December 1915, but, as a married man already over 40, he was not called up until 30 June 1916. Having been a Territorial for many years, he quickly found himself serving in the 2nd Battalion of the Hampshire Regiment in France. But he spent much time in and out of hospitals, resulting in his transfer to the 605th Agricultural Company of the Labour Corps.

Emily Bunch's family closely mirrors the national statistic that about one-in-eight men who served in the First World War did not return home.

***

The first attestation in 1915 from a Yateley address had been that of Harold Lovell Pennock. His record demonstrates another facet of wartime Yateley: that wives of serving men took short-term leases in Yateley, probably hoping to be close to their husbands if they were at Aldershot, Farnborough or Sandhurst. Mrs Anita Harston Pennock had married her husband on 3 December 1914 in the British Consulate in Bahia Blanca in Argentina. Forty-seven days later, her husband was in Whitehall, London, being attested as a draughtsman into the Royal Engineers, giving his wife's address as Dixie Cottage, Yateley. One year and 149 days later (15 June 1916), having served in the 17th Signals Company in France, Sapper Pennock took a commission in the Royal Engineers, when his wife's address was given as Lavender Cottage, Old Bracknell, Berkshire.

Most Yateley men who joined the Royal Navy in 1915 were new recruits, but William Filmore, who rejoined on 17 June 1915, had previously served for ten years from 1898. His service number was just one digit higher than that of Mark Hammond, who had been killed in action at the Battle of Coronel on 1 November 1914. They were born five months apart in 1882, both lived on Cricket Hill and they joined the Royal Navy on the same day. Neither of them appears on the Yateley Village School registers, although the several sisters of both of them were registered. William Filmore died at the age of 40 in 1923 and is buried in St Peter's churchyard. His father and mother, George and Harriet, baptized eight other children at St Peter's over a twenty-one year period. Another of their sons, James Filmore, five years older than William, also served in the Royal Navy and is listed in the *Hants & Berks Gazette* Roll of Honour of Christmas 1914 serving on HMS *Glory*. James and his wife, May née Ives, took over the tenancy of Staplen's Cottage on Potley Hill when his father-in-law became the publican of the Cricketers. He was a brother-in-law of George Ives, whose memoirs have been quoted. After William Filmore died, James married his brother's widow. James' own wife, May, had died in 1921.

Clifford George Sealy joined the Royal Navy on 25 August 1915 as a boy aged 16. There is an entry in the logbook of Yateley Village School for 1 March 1916:

> *'I hear ex-Warspite boys are making good progress*
> *Hilton & Lailey Merchant Service*
> *C Sealey Royal Navy*
> *Hilton took two prizes on Warspite. Sealey was acting quarter master.*
> *Hilton is quite a lad & is earning good money.*

Clifford Sealy had entered the local school in September 1904 when he was 4½. He left aged 14 on 25 July 1913. His younger brother, Victor, left on the same date, having won a scholarship to Robert May Grammar School in Odiham. Clifford went straight to TS *Warspite*. John Carter, the headmaster, was very keen on sending his boys to *Warspite*, which was a training ship run by the Marine Society providing a two-year apprenticeship to prepare poor boys of good character for the Royal Navy or the merchant service. Clifford Sealy's father was the Stilwells' coachman and lived at Hilfield Lodge, a close neighbour of James Filmore. From 23 June 1916 to 30 May 1918, Clifford Sealy served on HMS *Colossus*, the same ship as William Filmore.

The Shell Crisis
In early 1915, the government realized that the conflict was developing into a major war of attrition. The British Expeditionary Force was the relatively small army of regulars sent to France in August 1914. It had been reinforced by Regular Army battalions brought back from all corners of the Empire, replaced by Territorials like the 2/4th Hants in Quetta, India. The Regulars had not yet been reinforced by Kitchener's New Armies, still training, for example, on Yateley Common. By April, the BEF was already running out of shells, and it was realized that a war of attrition would require many more men than originally envisaged by Kitchener when he mobilized his New Armies through voluntary recruitment.

Conscription, the ultimate solution to the second problem, would, in 1916, have a profound impact on all Yateley families, but the critical immediate need was to put British industry on a total-war footing, and that would have a major effect on the career of one Yateley resident.

The first major turning point in the government's management of the war resulted from a combination of the First Sea Lord's resignation following disagreements with Churchill over the disastrous Gallipoli campaign and newspaper headlines claiming there was a 'shell crisis' on the Western Front. Liberal Prime Minister Asquith agreed with Bonar Law to form the first wartime coalition government. The major change in direction was the formation of the Ministry of Munitions under Lloyd George, wresting control of shells and weaponry from the War Office.

American company Holt made 'caterpillars' for hauling larger guns etc. They licensed other companies to meet the huge demand. The 'caterpillars' passed through Yateley on their way to the front. This postcard was sent on 20 July 1915 by Rose, his future wife, to Lance Corporal John Henry George Spence T/30539, serving with No.280 Auxiliary HT Company, Army Service Corps, in Rouen. She wrote: 'M D H [my dear heart] *I am wondering how you are I hope better. This was taken in the village by the post office. It has been a glorious day. With best love, Rose.' The couple were from the Isle of Wight. It is not known why she was in Yateley. Rose was a children's nurse. (Philip Todd)*

From a single table, in an otherwise empty building at 6 Whitehall Gardens, Lloyd George set about establishing a ministry which, by the end of the war, had 25,000 employees, mostly women, organized into fifty departments directly managing 250 government factories and supervising another 20,000 'controlled' establishments. By 1918, 61 per cent of the entire male industrial labour force was employed in war work of some kind, an even more striking percentage considering that the new National Factories were staffed mainly by women. Lloyd George realized he needed men of proven ability to undertake the transformation of industry into this large and efficient means of producing munitions.

One of these men was Sir Charles Stewart-Wilson, then recently retired from senior positions in the Indian Civil Service. Having returned to England, he had leased Yateley Manor and its parkland from Captain Richard Geaves. In 1914, Sir Charles had been a member of the committee appointed to reorganize the British Telegraph Service. Lloyd George swiftly appointed Sir Charles to be Assistant Secretary at the new Ministry of Munitions, a post he held until the Ministry of Munitions ceased to be. In today's terms, his Civil Service role would be Director.

A motor car standing in front of the Manor House. This picture, posed for the postcard, raises several issues: motor cars were rare; lady drivers even rarer; the young man is clearly an extra. Could this lady be Mrs Geaves, Lady Stewart-Wilson or a visitor to the Manor when it was a Red Cross Depot? (Jean McIlwaine)

Kitchener was the first serving officer ever to be appointed as Secretary of State for War. He realized, and stated in August 1914, that the war would last at least three years. His New Armies were trained accordingly, many regiments in them not being sent to France until they had trained for a year.

With voluntary recruitment falling away, Kitchener appointed Lord Derby as Director General of Recruiting on 11 October 1915. Five days later, Derby introduced the so-called 'Derby Scheme', made possible quickly because the National Registration Act of 15 July 1915 had determined the names and addresses of all men and women aged between 15 and 65, and recorded their employment skills.

The Derby Scheme gave men until 11 December to choose between voluntarily enlisting immediately, or to defer being called up. In either case, they had to go through the process of attesting. Attestation consisted of swearing allegiance to the monarch, and being formally accepted into the armed service. The third possibility was not to turn up at all.

The group who attested, but chose to defer being mobilized, were transferred to the Army Reserve and called up successively during 1916 according to their age and married status. Only 215,000 volunteered for immediate service, over two million chose to defer service and almost a million were classed in 'starred' (reserved) occupations. The scheme was a failure because, of those not in starred occupations, 38 per cent of single men and 54 per cent of married men – that is well over two million men – refused to register voluntarily under the Derby Scheme. Conscription became inevitable.

Of the five million who were eligible to attest voluntarily, over one million left it until the last few days before the Derby Scheme closed. Arthur Maurice Grainger, aged 26, of Vigo Lane was one who attested on 11 December 1915 for immediate service. He was posted to the 1st Battalion Hampshire Regiment, but shortly after he arrived in France in the following July he was transferred to the 1st Battalion Dorset Regiment. He was wounded in the forearm by a shell at St Quentin just seven days before the end of the war. On Armistice Day, he found himself at the University War Hospital in Southampton, spending over four months there before he was finally discharged from the Army.

Another man who left signing up until the last moment was 39-year-old William Charles Sackley of Ivy Cottage, Frogmore. He attested the day before Arthur Grainger. He too must have been wounded, because we only know his attestation date from his Silver Badge award. In 1915, William Sackley had not lived in Yateley for long, but he continued to live here for the rest of his life. He was buried in St Peter's churchyard in 1946, aged 70.

The Derby Scheme ran only from 16 October to 11 December 1915. In that time, five Yateley men attested into the Royal Flying Corps. One of them was George James Dymott, who was then living with his wife, Emilia, at Moorside Villas. He was attested on 26 November but was not called up for service until 5 March 1917, as an engineering fitter with rank Air Mechanic 1st Class. George Dymott had moved to Yateley from Eversley, a reminder of how closely related the two villages were during the war.

Tragic Drowning in the Blackwater
Before the war, Dymott had been the living-in head servant and head gardener at Kits Croft in Eversley. This large house of twenty-four rooms was the home of Major Alexis Charles Doxat, who had been awarded the Victoria Cross in the Boer War. Doxat was a member of the Stock Exchange. His father was Edmund T. Doxat, the Chairman of Dalgety & Co. Ltd, the largest importer of wool into the United Kingdom. The Doxat and Tindal families, the largest Australian meat canners of next-door Firgrove, were well acquainted.

Major Doxat re-enlisted to serve in his old regiment during the war, but found time on 10 September 1915 to purchase Monteagle Farm from Mrs Henrietta Ward, the wife of a Vicar of Marlow. Monteagle Farm comprised the 69 acres west of what we know call Monteagle Lane and north of the part of Yateley Common now known as Blackbushe Airport. Kits Croft adjoined this farm immediately across the Eversley/Yateley parish boundary. Mrs Ward was the sister of Miss Shute, who ran the Robins Grove estate including Mill Farm.

The tragic event which brought about the sale of Monteagle Farm was the drowning of Arthur Yeomans and his son. This was reported in *The Times* on 8 July 1915, but there was a much fuller account in the *Reading Mercury* of 10 July:

> '*Double Catastrophe: Father and Son Drowned at Yateley*
>
> '*On Sunday a little child, aged five years, the son of Arthur Yeomans, farmer of Yateley Mill farm, Sandhurst* [sic] *was playing near the Blackwater River when he fell in. His father jumped in after him to save him, but unfortunately both were drowned. The Hampshire and Berkshire police were soon upon the scene and commenced to drag the river, but they were unable to recover the bodies for over an hour. Owing to the bottom of the river, which is only twelve feet in depth at this point, being covered with branches of undergrowth, the bodies could not be extricated sooner, and it is also probable that Mr Yeomans got entangled in the undergrowth when he dived in to save his son.*
>
> '*The inquest was held on Wednesday. The evidence showed that another boy rushed indoors and told his father that his brother Ralph had fallen into the river near their home. Yeomans rushed out and jumped into the river, but sank and was drowned with his son.*'

In 1910, the year his son Ralph Lawrence had been baptized at St Peter's Yateley, Arthur Richard Yeomans had been the farm manager for Fir Grove Farm, part of the Kits Croft estate. His brother, Charles George, farmed Hawkins Farm next door. By 1915, Arthur Yeomans was managing Mill Farm in Yateley, owned by Miss Florence Shute of Robins Grove. The Shute family had been big landowners in Yateley, including Monteagle Farm, which Mrs Henrietta Ward had inherited separately from her eldest sister.

The death of Arthur Yeomans left Miss Shute without a farm manager at Mill Farm. The solution was for her sister to sell Monteagle Farm to Major Doxat so that Mrs Ward's bailiff at Monteagle, Edward White, could be transferred to manage Mill Farm. Not only did Edward White take over management of

Mill Farm, but he married Arthur Yeomans' widow at St Peter's on St Valentine's Day 1917.

Arthur Richard Yeomans was the son of Emma and Lawrence, a thatcher who had tried his hand at being the publican of The Royal Oak for three years in the late 1870s. Two of Arthur's brothers served in the First World War. Frederick Arthur Yeomans served on the home front as a farrier in the Army Veterinary Corps. Before the war, he owned a forge next-door to the Royal Oak. He died aged 48 in 1923. His brother, Charles George Yeomans, was a Derby Scheme man. He was attested on 26 November 1915 in Hartley Wintney and called up to serve in the Royal Berkshire Regiment on 20 June 1916. As a married man of 39 with a medical category of BII, he had been posted to the 12th (Labour) Battalion of the Berkshire Regiment, which had only been formed in Freshwater that June. The following month, he was shipped to France. When the Labour Corps was formed and absorbed the labour battalions of the county infantry regiments, Charles Yeomans was transferred to the 194th Company of the Labour Corps.

Casualties in 1915

At the same time that more men were continuing to volunteer or register under the Derby Scheme, some of those Yateley men who had gone cheerfully off to war in August 1914 were being wounded and others, sadly, were losing their lives.

The names of nine men killed in 1915 are inscribed on the Yateley War Memorial, but Company Sergeant Major Charles William Pryke is not named among them. A career soldier born in Warwickshire, he had married a Yateley girl at St Peter's on 1 November 1902 when he was a sergeant in the Oxfordshire Light Infantry. His bride was Mary Sophia, daughter of William and Sophia Hilton, and granddaughter of Isaac Hilton, a former parish clerk. The Hilton family had been created hereditary Parish Clerks by the then Perpetual Curate in 1809, and Henry Hilton was still parish clerk during the First World War. Mary Sophia later remarried and went to live in Australia. CSM Pryke was killed in action on 12 September 1915, serving with the 6th Battalion of his old regiment. This regiment was formed at Oxford in September 1914 as part of Kitchener's second New Army. They had only landed at Boulogne on 22 July 1915.

The mothers of two of those killed serving in the 4th Hants in Mesopotamia were at opposite ends of the social scale. Mrs Sylvia Macrae lived at Kerala with her husband, a colonel retired from commanding the Malibur Volunteer Rifles in Cochin, India, where he had worked as the managing director of a company growing and trading coffee, and representing such large organizations as Lloyds of London and Standard Vacuum Oil. Her husband died in 1920, but Mrs Macrae had already lost her eldest son, Charles Mackenzie Macrae, a young officer. His death on 5 July 1915 was widely reported in newspapers around the country, particularly in

After Mrs Sylvia Macrae died in 1935, Kerala was put up for auction. Above the mantelpiece in the lounge, a picture still hung of her son, Lieutenant Charles MacKenzie Macrae, killed in Mesopotamia on 5 July 1915 serving with the 1st/4th Hampshire Regiment. (Yateley Society Archive)

Kerala was built over several years from 1907 on an 11-acre field, originally part of West End Farm. Ellen Eggar from Farnham, a professional garden designer, laid out the gardens and parkland. The house was named after the Indian state where Alexander W. Macrae had lived for many years as a director of a trading company. He had also been Colonel of the Malabar Volunteer Rifles. Now demolished, the house was renamed The Haven in 1945, serving as a Baptist home for unmarried mothers until 1970. (Yateley Society Archive)

Scotland, as his grandfather was Dr Charles Mackenzie Macrae of Stornoway, sometimes referred to a the 'Grand Old Man of Lewis'.

Mrs Sophia Horne lived at Rose Cottage on Cricket Hill with her husband, James, a carter on a farm. She had sent her son to the village school on Yateley Green when he was 3 years and 4 months old. Private Jim Horne trained with the 4th Hants at Bustard Camp on Salisbury Plain before being shipped to India. He died from a head wound in Mesopotamia on 27 July 1915.

Yateley Funeral with full Military Honours
On 3 December, Yateley villagers witnessed a full military funeral for one of their young men. Sapper Archie Goodall was just 20 years old. He and his parents had not lived in Yateley for long. He had only married his wife earlier in 1915, on 3 April at Sandown, Isle of Wight, whilst he was serving with the Royal Engineers in Brading.

Archie joined the 7th Field Company RE in France on 15 May 1915 as part of an anti-aircraft searchlight unit. His billet in Armentières was shelled on the night of 12-13 September: he was one of the forty-five casualties.

The following is an extract from a newspaper cutting recently supplied to us by his family:

'YATELEY MILITARY FUNERAL – A most unusual and impressive sight in this village was witnessed on Friday, when the mortal remains of Sapper A. Goodall, late of the 7th Field Company were laid to rest in St. Peter's Churchyard with military honours. He was severely wounded by the explosion of a bomb on a house in Armentières, where he, with other comrades, was billeted, and was brought over from France to the County of London Hospital at Epsom. Here for a time he appeared to progress favourably, but complications set in, and he passed away peacefully on Tuesday Nov 30th, his young wife, with his father and mother, being present to soothe his last moments. The body was met at Blackwater Station by the band and firing party of the Royal Engineers from Aldershot, and the coffin, covered with a Union Jack, was placed on a gun carriage and was taken to Yateley, a distance of some three miles, where his father and mother reside. Here a large and sympathetic crowd awaited the procession, the band playing Chopin's Funeral March, and the firing party marching with arms reversed. The body was met at the lych gate by the Vicar (Reverend J. Beardall, MA, RD), who most impressively conducted the funeral service, the choir also being present ... The service at the grave being ended, the firing party fired three volleys over the grave, the concluding bars of the Dead March in 'Saul' being played by the band between each volley, and then the trumpeter sounded 'The Last Post.' The scene was most solemn and yet most inspiring – a Grand Finale to one who laid down his life for King and Country. It should stimulate all young men to go and 'do their bit' and so bring this awful war to an early conclusion.'

CHAPTER 3

1916

The Military Service Act 1916 was given royal assent on 27 January. On 2 March 1916, every male resident in Great Britain who was unmarried, or a widower without dependent children on 15 November 1915, would be deemed, with certain exemptions, 'to have been duly enlisted in His Majesty's regular forces for general service with the colours or in the reserve for the period of the war, and to have been forthwith transferred to the reserve', provided they had reached the age of 18 on 15 August 1915, and had not reached the age of 41. The Derby Scheme had failed to provide enough new recruits. Conscription had arrived.

Had you been travelling through Yateley on Wednesday, 27 January 1916 along the main road from Reading to Aldershot, what would you have seen? There were no buses, and very few people owned cars. You were unlikely to have been in a pony and trap, as most horses had been requisitioned by the Army Remount Centre in Arborfield, which you would already have passed through.

You would probably have walked the 12 miles from Reading, unless you owned a bicycle. So there would have been plenty of time to take in a great amount of detail as you walked from the Eversley/Yateley parish boundary through the village to reach Yateley Lodge at the junction with Cricket Hill Lane.

Eversley Lane
Perhaps you had with you a copy of the latest Ordnance Survey map published in 1911. If you only had the previous issue published in 1894, you would have been surprised to find the road now lined with

houses on each side directly before and after the parish boundary. Many of these houses have date-stones still clearly visible showing they were built just before and after 1900.

On the south side of the road, you would have passed No.1 Hawthorn Cottages, where you could have passed the time of day with Alice English, the wife of Joseph Herbert English, a house painter. She might have told you that her 18-year-old son, Lawrence Herbert, had just joined the Royal Marines the previous month. He was a carpenter and had been immediately posted as a sapper to Deal in Kent. In October 1917, the Marines would receive a War Office order to transfer him to the Royal Engineers. Sadly, he died in 1922 of pulmonary tuberculosis, known as consumption, a common cause of death of young adults at that time.

Sapper English was the grandson of Thomas English, who owned and farmed Moor Place Farm. Thomas' wife, Susannah, from Shoreham in Sussex, first appeared in the Yateley census is 1881. Thomas, also born in Shoreham, was not at home on census night 1881, but Susannah described herself as 'ropemaker's wife'. Ten years later, Thomas was at home on census night and described himself as a dairy farmer. It was workmen digging a gravel pit in 1926 for Thomas and Susannah's son, Bartlett W English, who would discover the Bronze Age funerary urns on Moor Place Farm, resulting in local people now calling the farm 'the Urnfield'.

Leaving behind you the turn-of-the-century houses in Eversley Lane, Yateley Green starts to open out in front of you. Yateley villagers of January 1916 called it The Common, and the 1,000 acres of heathland we now call Yateley Common, they called Hartfordbridge Flats, but the Ordnance Survey named Yateley's common land Yateley Green and Yateley Common, just as we do. Both areas are now registered as common land under the 1965 Act. A new road was constructed across Yateley Green in 1801, so your imaginary walk in 1916 presents you with a choice: left or right fork?

Vicarage Road

The left fork is the ancient route from Reading, skirting the northern edge of The Green. Today there are houses built all along the left-hand side of this old road, now called Vicarage Road. In 1916, you would not have seen the 'Homes for Heroes' built after the Great War. There were no houses after you left the 1900s housing on Eversley Lane until you reached a house on the eastern corner of the junction with Moulsham Lane leading to Moor Place. This first house, called Mostyn Cottage, was built by James Bunch in 1879, and he still lived in it in 1916. After the war, he advertised his house as apartments.

Mrs Brown, the widow of Colonel V.C.M. Brown VC, was living in an apartment at Mostyn Cottage in 1916, since she gave Yateley as her address when notices of the death at Gallipoli of her son, Captain Wynyard Keith Brown, appeared in national and local papers in June 1915. She was first recorded at her new residence on Cricket Hill in the Electoral Registers of spring 1920. She was probably living alone in 1916, as her daughter, Jessie, was nursing elsewhere, and 'Llewyn', her youngest son, was interned in Germany.

James Bunch was one of the brothers who had carved the screen in St Peter's Church which unfortunately was destroyed in the 1979 fire. He was the youngest of the thirteen children of William and Mary Ann Bunch. Two of his elder brothers, Aaron and Henry, owned all the other houses on Vicarage Road except the last three. The Hollies and Goose Green Cottage were owned by the Misses Ellis. The largest house, on the corner of Chandlers Lane, was The Poplars, which in 1916 was the residence of Mrs Charrington.

If you had popped your head into the Bunchs' workshop on Vicarage Road, they would probably have told you that labour was getting very scarce. The brothers had been house builders before the war. The younger men who had been their bricklayers, plasterers, plumbers and labourers, many of them working on their own account as journeymen, had by now either volunteered for war service or were waiting to be called-up under the Derby Scheme.

The Bunch brothers might also have told you that William Tice the baker, who also sold groceries from his little shop in a wooden hut in the front garden of Goose Green Cottage, was then in a similar position. His youngest son was a policeman and had just volunteered, and his middle son had already spent years in the Royal Navy. Mr Tice's eldest son, Harold Ernest, who was running the business with him before the war, had been a sergeant with the Surrey Yeomanry and, as a territorial, had immediately been called up in August 1914. He was now a quartermaster sergeant in the East Surrey Regiment.

Mrs Charrington had only recently moved into the imposing house called The Poplars, next-door to Goose Green Cottage. It had cost £2,000 in 1897 when it had been built on the site of an ancient farm called Gales Farm. While she was living in Lewes, Isabella Charrington had lost her younger son, Captain Arthur Craven Charrington. He had been killed in France in October 1914 serving with the 1st Royal Dragoon Guards, part of the Household Cavalry. His father, Nicholas, was from the famous Charrington Brewery family, and had worked as a brewer in the early part of his adult life. Mrs Charrington's elder son was Captain Edward Somerset Charrington, serving at the Remount Depot at Swathling, near Southampton. He had inherited Bures Manor, near Reigate, which had been the family estate since the sixteenth century.

Looking across Yateley Green towards Vicarage Road. In centre of the photograph, at the the top of Chandlers Lane, is The Poplars, now demolished. At the far left-hand side is William Burroughs Tice's bakery and shop in the front gardens of his house, Goose Green Cottage, now a listed building. The pond has now been filled in. (Richard Johnston)

The Poplars was built in 1897 on the site of an ancient farm called Gales Farm. The site is now a cul-de-sac called Crondall End. The land-use of this site is typical of Yateley's development: an ancient farmstead replaced by a mansion house standing during the two world wars, itself replaced by a modern housing estate.

The Military Hospital

To continue your journey towards the centre of Yateley, you would have walked across the neck of Yateley Green, which extended down to Chandlers Farm. Once across it, you would have reached Yateley Auxiliary Military Hospital, run by the Red Cross and staffed by two or three professional nurses plus a team of local ladies from the Hampshire Voluntary Aid Detachment 94. In normal times, this large house was Yateley's vicarage, but in 1916 it was a hive of activity.

Perhaps, on your imaginary walk, you would meet Mrs Petrie, the doctor's wife, as she hurried on one of the many trips she made between her home at Barclay House next door and the Vicarage. Dr Alexander Sturrock Petrie was the doctor for the hospital, which included the ward at Fir Grove in Eversley. Tragically, he died in September 1917 aged only 39. Mrs Sophy Williamina Hope Petrie was a Scot, six years older than her husband. The eulogy at Dr Petrie's funeral, as reported in the *Reading Mercury*, also recorded the devoted service Mrs Petrie gave to Yateley Military

The Rev Beardall and his wife moved out of the Vicarage so that it could become a military hospital run by the Red Cross detachment of local ladies. Coming under Aldershot Command, the wounded soldiers were transferred to Yateley after initial treatment at the Cambridge and Connaught Hospitals. (Philip Todd)

Hospital. The patients from Yateley and Eversley hospitals attended Dr Petrie's funeral, as did the nurses, VADs and doctors.

The hospital's cook, Miss Ruth Alderman, would lose her only son, Percy Allen Alderman, killed in Mesopotamia on 21 January 1916 serving with the 1/4th Hants. Ruth Alderman was an unmarried mother living with her brother in Mill Lane. Percy had been born in Sandhurst in 1895. On his birth certificate his father's name had been left blank, but his surname was given as Allen. In later life, he was always known as Percy Alderman. Mrs Petrie might also have told you about the many Yateley ladies who were giving freely many hours nursing the wounded soldiers, including Mrs Aida Norris and Miss Mary Le Mesurier, who lived at Shane Cottage, one of the Bunch houses which you have just passed on Vicarage Road.

Walking on from the vicarage, you will see a shed in its garden before you reach Barclay House. This shed was the office of Yateley Parish Council, its position in the garden of the vicarage reflecting the fact that before 1894 the parish council had been under the aegis of the Established Church.

Written on the back of this postcard are the names of each nurse in the photograph, including two professional nurses, Sister Findlay and Sister K. Murray. (Jean McIlwaine)

You might even meet the Vicar, the Rev Beardall, as he was then living at Simla, just three houses nearer to the village. Simla was one of the four houses between the vicarage and the White Lion which had been owned in the early nineteenth century by Herbert Lewis, a draper with a business in Reading. Barclay House, The White House, Simla and Harpton House were now owned by a family trust. From time to time, members of the family lived in one or other of the houses, but mostly they were leased to others, such as to Dr Petrie at Barclay House. Simla had recently been rebuilt. That building still stands today, renamed Gayton House. Until January 1914, it had been leased by Mr A.H. Templer, but that month he had purchased Holly Hill from the executors of John Mills. Simla was therefore still vacant when war broke out. The Rev Beardall had moved to Simla to enable the vicarage to become the wartime hospital.

The White House stood next-door to Barclay House until the 1970s. It was a big, old, comfortable-looking rambling house and was Herbert Lewis's own home. During the First World War, it was the home of the Rev George Herbert Oakshott and his wife. The Roll of Honour in St Peter's Church states that he was a naval chaplain

A view across Yateley Green which, confusingly, in the First World War was called Yateley Common. The 1,000 acres we now call Yateley Common was then more usually called Hartfordbridge Flats, from which the Second World War airfield took its name before it was renamed RAF Blackbushe in 1945. The houses in the picture are those along Vicarage Lane from the Vicarage to Harpton House. (Richard Johnston)

during the war. He was chaplain aboard HMS *Endymion* when it was in action at Cape Hellas during the Gallipoli campaign. On Sunday 18 July 1915, on his 47th birthday, he held divine service aboard HMS *Endymion* at Port Mudros, the main Allied base for the Gallipoli campaign. He transferred to the hospital ship HMHS *Gascon* on 28 July 1915, but by 10 August he was aboard HMS *Exmouth*, the only battleship allowed to maintain station off the Gallipoli beaches after three other battleships had been sunk within two weeks. Later in the war, the Rev Oakshott became chaplain at the Royal Navy base at Chatham. From 1917-1918, he was chaplain to the military hospital at Minley.

The Vicarage, Barclay House and The White House were three of the six Yateley houses originally listed in 1952 as having special architectural and historical interest. Unfortunately, before it became illegal to do so, The White House was left empty for some time so that it deteriorated to such an extent that the District Council was asked to condemn it and it was demolished.

WHITE HOUSE, YATELEY.

During the Great War, the White House on Vicarage Road was the home of Rev George Herbert Oakshott DD and his wife, Edith. The house was listed Grade II in 1952, but subsequently bought by a developer, left vacant and allowed to deteriorate, before it was illegal to do so. The house was condemned as unfit for human habitation and then demolished. (Malcolm Miller)

As you were standing talking to the Vicar outside Simla, you might have glanced south across the main road. Hall Lane had not been straightened in those days to form the crossroad with Village Way, which then caused the roundabout to be built in the 1980s. The route in 1916 ran passed the front gate of Yateley Court, which was then called Holm Dene. There were no buildings on the south side of the main road between Holm Dene on Hall Lane and the Dog & Partridge.

Harpton House stood between Simla (Gayton House) and the White Lion. The house was demolished in the 1960s in order to create Village Way. Mrs Susan Mary Chapman lived at Harpton House from before 1891 until her death in 1936. Her husband, a retired Crown Surveyor, had died in 1900. He was one of the Chapman family who owned the four Lewis Trust houses on Vicarage Lane. Mrs Chapman was the aunt of Paul Nash, the famous war artist of the Great War.

During his childhood, Paul Nash lived with his Aunt Susan in Yateley, attending Mrs Wilding's private school for girls on Cricket

A view of Church End Green from outside the gate of Harpton House. Mrs Susan Mary Chapman, who lived at Harpton House during the First World War, was the widowed aunt of Paul Nash, the famous war artist. Nash was a frequent visitor both before and after the war. As a young boy he lived with his aunt in Yateley for a time and attended a private girls' school, Mrs Wilding's, on Cricket Hill. (Philip Todd)

The Vicarage on Yateley Green to The Croft at Church End, Yateley.

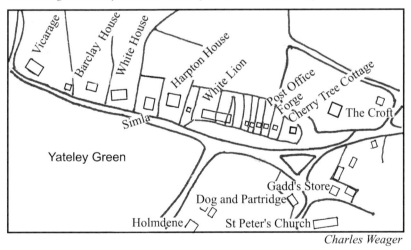

Charles Weager

Hill as the only boy. Mrs Wilding was very keen on teaching her girls to paint. One of her daughters had time off from teaching at the school to attend Reading School of Art, the founding school of the present university. As an adult, Paul Nash was a regular visitor to Harpton House both before and after the First World War.

The Village

Now you have reached the White Lion, you might go inside for some refreshment. George Higgs had been proprietor since 1903. In 1916, he would be very pleased to see you as his business was very bad. Many of his pre-war customers were already away serving with the forces and, although the area was awash with training battalions, he could be prosecuted for serving alcohol to servicemen. The following is an extract from Valerie Kerslake's oral history notes:

> *'Distraught, he had to tell his eldest son that he could no longer afford to keep him at home. A post was found for the son, aged 14, as hall boy in a large house near London, and this was the start of a spectacular career in service in which he was eventually working as butler in some of the grandest establishments in the country. Meanwhile George Higgs added geese and more poultry to the cow and hens he already kept behind the pub to try to augment his income.'*

A postcard in the Bettesworth series, posted on 25 May 1907. It shows the mail delivery car outside Bettesworth Post Office and gives a good impression of the openness of Yateley Green at that time. (Philip Todd)

YATELEY VILLAGE.   Bettesworth, Yateley.

The centre of the old village only extended from the White Lion to the Plough, but included St Peter's Church, the Manor House and the Dog & Partridge all stretching back to time immemorial. The White Lion and the Plough were new pubs compared with the Dog & Partridge, which had until 1888 been owned by the church. In 1912, the brewery, which now owned it, completely demolished the old building, rebuilding in the modern road-house style dominating the little triangle of grass in front of the old church lych gate.

The centre of Yateley in 1916, then sometimes known as Church End, and at other times as simply 'the village', would have appeared completely differently from today. There was no tarmacadam, no kerbs, no street lighting and definitely no traffic lights. The unmade roads had been kept in a reasonable state of repair before the war by roadmen working for Hartley Wintney Rural District Council. Many of those men had volunteered for the Army, which itself was using the main road for tracked vehicles, steam-propelled lorries and the newer light lorries with internal combustion engines, causing increasing wear and tear on the gravelled surfaces.

The centre of Yateley would have seemed quite busy to local people during the First World War, but to us, without the constant flow of two-way traffic and cars parked in all available spaces, the Yateley of 1916 would have appeared much like a rural backwater. The passing of a privately owned car would then have caused people to look up to see to whom it belonged.

Mrs Masterman, Sydney Loader's father's employer living at Heathcroft, did have a car and a chauffeur. Sydney Loader recalls in his memoirs:

> *I well remember my first car ride. I was nine, Captain Masterman had died* [in July 1915] *and their chauffeur had to go somewhere just as I was going to school. He gave me a lift to school and for the first and probably the only time, I was first there.*

There were perhaps only ten motor cars in the entire village. The Hudson family had been 'fly-proprietors' operating from a building

A postcard of the view westwards towards the White Lion, posted in June 1913 when the sight of a motor car on the main road was still something of a rarity. (Gordon Harland)

jutting out from the left-hand side of the White Lion. In the 1915 edition of *Kelly's Directory*, Ed Hudson was still describing himself as a 'jobmaster', 'a man who keeps a livery stable and lets out horses and carriages by the job'. Just before the war, the Hudsons started a motor taxi service. That made one of his sons, Thomas Butler Hudson, a prime candidate for service as an army driver. He had joined up under the Derby Scheme in November 1915. His younger brother, William George Hudson, joined the Army Veterinary Corps. He was another Yateley man who served in Salonika, where he died in January 1919.

Continue your journey eastwards from the White Lion. You will notice a shop at the right end of the building. This was a general store then, used mainly by ordinary families. The gentry tended to use Gadd & Co's Yateley Supply Store across the Green to the left of the church lych gate. The distinction was that before the war, Gadd's ran a home delivery service to the large houses, not only in Yateley but in the surrounding villages. Throughout the war, Gadd's was managed by Edmund Charles Webley and his wife, Florence. They were not locals and had previously managed shops elsewhere. Webley sold one of the series of postcards on which we rely now for images of this period.

The other series of postcards from this period was sold by William Bellingham Bettesworth, the postmaster. After William Gadd had retired to Littlehampton, Bettesworth had taken over management of Gadd's stores. He also took over from Gadd the position of being Yateley's postmaster. As postmaster in 1901,

Gadd's Stores. Yateley.

This postcard of delivery carts outside The Yateley Supply Stores, otherwise known as Gadd's Stores, was posted on 8 June 1909. (Malcolm Miller)

Bettesworth had employed, as the operator of his telegraph machine, Flora Timms, later better known by her married name as the authoress Flora Thompson. In 1903, Bettesworth decided to take the Post Office business over the road, renting a very old house called Trythes, and Webley took over then as Gadd's manager at the Yateley Supply Stores.

Until 1965, all the houses between the White Lion and the smithy had remained as separate buildings, detached or semi-detached. During the redevelopment of Yateley following the Second World War, it was decided to join all these buildings into one long row, renaming them Sadlers Court and Forge Court to give some idea of their previous history.

As you walk eastwards from the White Lion, and before you reach the Post Office, you will pass two more local businesses. In the year before the war, Newman & Sons, saddlers of Crowthorne, had established a branch of their business in the front room of one of the houses. The Hilton family had also been established there as boot and shoemakers for over a century. Henry Hilton, then 78 years old, was the head of the family, and one of the best-known villagers. For forty-seven years, he had been parish clerk of Yateley church, and had served under five vicars. He had been Yateley's parish clerk before the Local Government Act 1894 had established elected parish councils and separated local government from the Established Church. Henry Hilton, who had dealt with both, could certainly have told you a thing or two about Yateley's history.

Trythes, where in 1916 William Bettesworth now ran the Post Office, had for centuries been the home of the village blacksmith. From the early eighteenth century, the forge had been run by members of the Bunch family. In 1877, both Trythes and the forge next door had been purchased by J.P. Stilwell. In 1916, John Hawkins was the blacksmith.

To the east of the forge, Cherry Tree Cottage had been a pair of small thatched cottages where successive families of cordwainers had lived. In 1912, the old cottages were pulled down and a pair of new semi-detached houses was built by Arthur Henry Templer. He was the retired tea-planter who had previously lived at Simla, and before that at Heathcroft. In 1916, he was Chairman of the Yateley Parish Council, living at Holly Hill.

Yateley Post Office was run by William Bellingham Bettesworth during the Great War. His wife was the sister of Frank Bridge, the composer. A close-up of the window to the left of the door reveals the postcard collection, many of which are used to illustrate this book. The house, known as Trythes, is now incorporated into Forge Court. It was mentioned in the Crondal Customary of 1567, and was for centuries the home of the blacksmith who ran the forge next-door to the right. (Jean McIlwaine)

One side of Cherry Tree Cottage housed the telephone exchange and the other the police constable. The telephone exchange was in the front room of Frank Strange's house. Frank's son, Alfred Frank Strange, was always known as Charlie. He is recorded on the St Peter's Church First World War Roll of Honour serving in the Hampshire Regiment as Charles Strange. His 17th birthday was on 17 January 1916, but he had joined up under-age, and served in the 2/4th Battalion of the Royal Berkshire Regiment.

The Cherry Tree Cottages were built on land which had been part of the Manor Farm. Templer was a second cousin to the Mason ladies still living in the village. The old Manor Farmhouse faced the church across the small green which formed the centre of the old village. After Captain George Mason died in 1887, his executors sold most of the manor to Captain Richard Lyon Geaves, but the Mason family retained ownership of the Manor Farmhouse and some land around it. It was renamed The Croft, and in 1916 was the home of the three elderly unmarried daughters of George Mason. At the end of the war, they would gift a small site from their front garden for the Yateley War Memorial.

Looking across the main road from where the War Memorial is now erected to the left of Yateley Supply Stores, you will see an old house which is probably the oldest still existing in Yateley. In 1916, it was called St Peter's Cottage. Now it is the Grade II listed building called Ye Olde Vicarage, because it served as the vicarage for a few years around the Second World War. In 1916, it too was the home of an elderly spinster from a family which had lived in Yateley for more than a century.

When the Vicar buried Miss Ellen Caswall on 24 November 1917, he noted in the register that she was 'Grand daughter of a former Vicar of Yateley'. That vicar was the Rev Robert Clarke Caswall, who had built the Vicarage at his own expense in the early 1800s and which was, in 1916, being used as the Yateley Military Hospital.

Continuing your journey eastwards, you will reach The Manor House on your right. Lady Stewart-Wilson had volunteered the Manor as Hospital Supply Depot No.1133. This large private house

This photograph was taken before 1900 from the south across the fields from an old path which is now Cranford Park Drive. The buildings to the left of the church include the ancient tithe barn and the butcher's shop run by John Hills. Before the new Vicarage was built in the 1800s, this shop had been the Parsonage. This view gives a particularly fine sense of the centre of the village. (Richard Johnston)

was one of more than 2,700 Red Cross supply depots across the country, the next nearest being Blackwater House, the home of Mrs Grace Agnes Carrington. She was the sister of Brigadier General Arthur Douglas Lumley, who had commanded No.10 District (ie Surrey) before the war.

If you turn your back on the Manor House, you will be able to see across the open meadow to Coronation Road, the first new road to be constructed in Yateley since the main road was cut across the Green in 1801. Bertie Alfred Fullbrook was the man behind this new development, which was named for the coronation of King George V in 1911. From the Green eastwards, the main road was called Blackwater Road during the First World War.

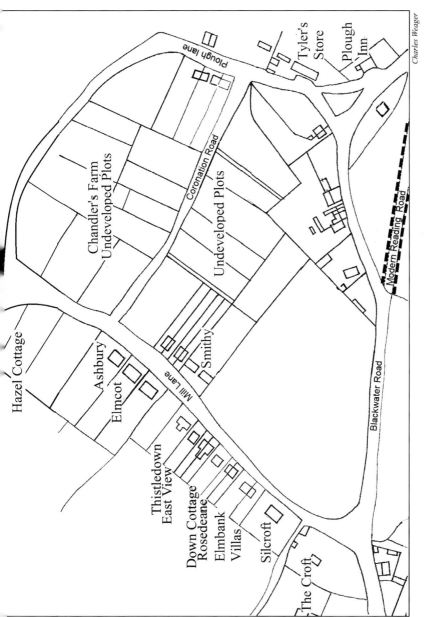

Charles Weager

The Mill Lane development plots are shown here as recorded on the maps accompanying the 1910 Land Tax assessments. By 1919, the Electoral Registers listed twenty-one parliamentary voters living on the newly built Coronation Road, including seven away on military service. Harry and Janet Mary Hawkins, living at Kirkee, had three sons away serving in the forces.

Walk on eastwards past the field which is now Yateley Industries for the Disabled. On the north side of the road was the workshop and home of the builder and master carpenter J.R. Bunch, whose son, Cyril, went on the bellringing expedition with one of the Butler boys from across the road.

In 1916, the main road did not continue straight as it does now: it followed the road now called Plough Road, past Knellers Cottages, past Tyler's Stores at the top of Plough Lane (now called Fry's Lane), past the Plough beer house - now the site of a supermarket – to pass in front of Rosebank Villas. The Butlers' cottage was right across the road from the Plough.

You will pass the home of Daniel and Emily Bunch, whose sons worked for J.R. Bunch, but were now away serving their country. They lived at No.2 Lewis's, an old house immediately on the left down Plough Lane. Tyler's Stores was across the road on the right-hand side of Plough Lane, now known as Fry's Lane. On Boxing Day 1892, James Robert Bunch, the builder, had married May Tyler, the daughter of George Boorer Tyler and his wife, Ruth. In 1878, Tyler had purchased from the Hawkins family their provisions business established in the house we now know as Little Halt. George Boorer Tyler had died in 1908, and Ruth was now 77. Ruth died in October 1916, but in May, Tyler's Stores was put on the market. The Tylers did not own the property, but their son, Harry, a baker by trade, had been running the business for years. In September 1916 J.P. Stilwell, the owner, sold the property to Thomas English of Moor Place Farm.

Thomas English, Bertie Fullbrook's father-in-law, was most probably interested in developing what the auctioneers called in the newspaper 'a small valuable piece or parcel of building land'. The shop must have continued in business, because Thomas English's executors sold it to Harold Ernest Tice in December 1921. Tice then went on to buy the Yateley Supply Stores next to the church and renamed it Tice's, becoming the main retailer in Yateley.

In January 1916, Albert Thomas Hearmon was 'mine host' at the Plough, but he was conscripted on 1 August. The pub became a typical example of a business kept going by a wife while her

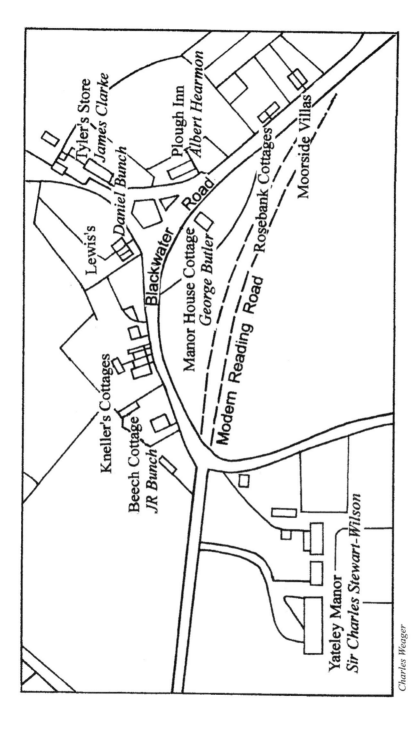

Charles Weager

The main road from the Manor House past the Plough Inn was not straightened until after the Second World War.

husband was away. Mrs Laura Hearmon became the licensee. She was the daughter of Jesse and Annie Bunch, and would eventually have three brothers serving in the army, although Ralph Bunch was not yet old enough in 1916 to be conscripted. She was destined to lose her brother-in-law after the war was officially over: William George Hearmon was serving in the Royal Army Veterinary Corps and is buried in Yateley churchyard.

Beyond the Plough on your left there were two sets of semi-detached villas. As you walked past Moorside Villas, it would have appeared that you were leaving the old village of Yateley. On both sides of the road there were then just open fields until you reached the Drill Hall. The fields to the south were still part of the Manor estate, and beyond them to the south had been the medieval strip fields. To the north of the road, the fields stretched down to the River Blackwater. Those fields nearest to the river had been managed as water meadows for centuries as they flooded every year.

By 1916, the Drill Hall, the home of F Company of the 4th Hants, had become a main social hub of the village. Behind it there was a small-bore rifle range used for military training. The range was also the home of the Yateley Ladies' Rifle Club, which had been started before the war by Miss Beatrice Stilwell, with help and advice from Miss Rose Kingsley.

According to the Hampshire Chronicle of 4 December 1909, after he had performed its opening ceremony in 1909 by firing the first shot down the range:

> 'Lord Basing finished an excellent address by saying that if the Rifle Clubs and the Territorials were thoroughly well supported universal service [conscription] will be unnecessary, the Rifle Clubs training the boys to shoot preparatory to joining the Territorials, and making the older men of use in an invasion.'

Earlier in 1909, at a recruiting meeting held at the Drill Hall, the perceived threat of invasion was put more graphically, as reported again by the *Hampshire Chronicle* on 13 March 1909:

The Drill Hall was erected in 1893 as the depot of the Yateley Company of the volunteer battalion of the Hampshire Regiment. It was built on land owned by J.P. Stilwell. This photograph is of an American car converted in the Second World War to be the first fire engine of the Yateley Brigade. The Drill Hall was destroyed by fire after the Second World War and the site became The Parade of modern shops. (the late Benjie Wilmer)

> *'One of the chief points in Major Naish's speech was that in the event of invasion, all the young men who had not fitted themselves to defend their country would be left with the women and children under a white flag, a very inglorious position for an able-bodied young man, for which he would be held up to ridicule afterwards. Cpt. White of Fleet made a very practical speech, and said Englishmen do not realise what invasion means, with its consequent horrors, or he was sure the young men of England would willingly give their services for the defence of their country and homes.'*

The Royal Oak is still a licensed premises opposite the junction with the road to Sandhurst. A pre-war photograph indicates there was a large smithy on its left-hand side, run by Fred Yeoman, with up to seven employees including Fred Bull. Fred Bull had finished his apprenticeship as a blacksmith with George Parker in Darby Green when he had joined the Army Service Corps in 1906. However, he was discharged almost immediately as 'not likely to become an efficient soldier'. During the Great War, he re-enlisted in the army, becoming a farrier sergeant in the Army Veterinary Corps.

The licensee of the Royal Oak was Arthur Ernest White. In 1911, he had been a cab driver at a livery stables, probably the one run by the Hudson family at the White Lion. By 1915, he had taken over running the pub. He had been born in Axminster, so was not a member of the White family which had lived in Yateley since the thirteenth century.

The Royal Oak and its smithy were well situated to cater for the passing trade on the main Reading to Aldershot road, as well as for travellers coming from Sandhurst, Wokingham and Reading heading for Fleet and Farnham by going up Cricket Hill. The main road continued on to Darby Green, Blackwater and eventually London or Aldershot.

Your imaginary journey on 27 January 1916 will now take you past Yateley Lodge at the bottom of Cricket Hill at its junction with Blackwater Road. Mrs Constance Wood, the owner of Yateley Lodge, was very ill in January 1916 and would die on 20 March that year. Her eldest daughter from her first marriage, Miss Constance Margaret Marx, lived with her.

This postcard from the Bull family album in Canada shows Fred Bull at the extreme left of the picture. Frederick Yeoman's smithy was to the left of the Royal Oak, which in 1915 was run by Arthur Ernest White and his wife, Mary Ann. Henry Hewett & Co Ltd of Waltham St Lawrence, founded in 1842, had supplied beer to the Royal Oak since before 1862. (Linda Davis)

Miss Margaret Marx had been involved with the Red Cross Hants 94 Voluntary Aid unit from when it was formed in 1909, but was now raising funds for the Serbian Relief Fund. She had worked at Lady Cornelia Wimborne's Hospital in Skopje, Serbia for several months in 1915. On 19 January 1916, Miss Marx gave a lecture and slide show at the Central Hall in Camberley. One week before that lecture, she had arranged 'an entertainment' in Yateley's Drill Hall, also to raise funds for the Serbian Relief Fund. Her home, Yateley Lodge, will play a vital role in 1917.

The Big Battles of 1916

Apart from being the first year in recent British history that its citizens had been conscripted for military service, 1916 is also remembered for two big battles: the Battle of Jutland at sea and the Battle of the Somme on the Western Front. Graham Fleuty's book *Yateley Men at War: Heartbeats of Remembrance* tells the story of how those men listed on Yateley's War Memorial met their deaths fighting for their country. Reginald Legg, son of a blacksmith living on Mill Lane, was killed at Jutland on HMS *Invincible*, and Fred Grainger and Charles Callas Wooldridge were killed during the 141 days of the Battle of the Somme.

Yateley War Memorial commemorates those who were killed in the ecclesiastical parish of St Peter's Yateley, whereas this book tells the story of the Yateley Society's 'area of benefit' – the Civil Parish of Yateley. The parish of St Peter's was only two-thirds the size of the civil parish. At least five other men serving at Jutland had next-of-kin living here during the war, and one, Surgeon John Sides Davies MacCormac of Darby Green, was killed when HMS *Black Prince* was sunk. One more man serving at Jutland was born here, and another came to live here for the rest of his life shortly after the war. We can even claim a Yateley connection with Admiral Cecil Burney, the second-in-command of the Grand Fleet at the Battle of Jutland in his flagship HMS *Marlborough*. He was created a baronet in 1921. When he died in 1929, his widow and his son came to live in Yateley at Frogmore House.

Herbert Alfred Buckner lost his life on the third day of the Battle of the Somme. His name does not appear on Yateley War Memorial, although he attended Yateley Village School. As the Buckner family lived in Rosemary Lane in Frogmore, he is remembered in the Hawley Memorial Hall. At the time of his death, he was serving in the 2nd Battalion of the Hampshire Regiment.

Abraham and Jane Buckner had moved to Yateley from Wokingham to live in one of a pair of cottages built in 1901 and owned by John Brinn. Jane gave birth to fifteen children. All of them were alive in 1911, with eight still at home, including Alfred. During the war, seven of Alfred's brothers and at least one brother-in-law served in the armed forces. We believe therefore that Jane Buckner was the Yateley mother with the most sons serving in the war.

Atrocious Weather

In Yateley, living conditions were deteriorating. The bad weather did not help. The following is from the pocket book of William Burrows Tice:

> *Feb 23rd, 1916: Heavy snow began to fall and by the 25th and 26th more than one foot had fallen. Travelling very bad. Snow laid about until Sunday 12th March. No fall anything like it since 1908.*
>
> *March 28th, 1916: Severe Blizzard. Snow accompanied by N E wind, most severe since Jan 18th, 1881. Trees blown down, Telegraph and Telephone service quite suspended in some places owing to wires broken by falling trees etc.'*

William Burrows Tice, the baker and grocer who kept the shop at Goose Green Cottage, was a local reporter for the *Hants & Berks Gazette*. He kept a pocket book in which he pasted cuttings of his own articles, and some others relevant to Yateley. All comments he made in his own handwriting during the First World War were about the extremes in the weather.

Appealing against Conscription

Life too was getting much bleaker in 1916. Enforced conscription was beginning to bite into the labour supply which had been maintaining vital services and supplies for those remaining in the village. By September, W.B. Tice was advertising in the *Reading Mercury* for 'an experienced bread baker' who would be ineligible for call-up. Newspaper reports of the Appeals Tribunals held in Basingstoke show that by April, Yateley men, and their employers attempting not to lose key men, were appearing before the board in Basingstoke Town Hall.

At one such hearing on 3 May 1916, the *Reading Mercury* reported:

> '*F.W. English, Yateley, appealed on the grounds that he was the only cowman on a farm of 123 acres with 25 cows. In reply to Mr. Marley* [the military representative] *the appellant said the milk round had been sold, but they still had to produce the milk. His father, though old and deaf, could still do considerable work. – Allowed exemption till Sept. 1st.*'

Positively identifying this farm as Moor Place Farm, and the father as Thomas English, presents no problems. Thomas English died in Yateley Cottage Hospital on 4 October 1920, aged 77. Thomas and Susannah English had ten children, including Frederick, born in 1879, Bart, and Joseph who lived on Eversley Lane.

Frederick Charles English had left Yateley before 1901 to become a gardener for Alexander Henderson MP at Buscot Park in Berkshire. Frederick English had married Edith Bennett in Basingstoke in 1906. In 1911, he had been head gardener at Ellisfield Manor near Basingstoke. It is therefore unlikely that he was the appellant at the tribunal in May 1916, as married men with three dependent children had not yet been conscripted.

By 1911, only Bartlett William English was living at home in Yateley with his parents. His occupation in that census was 'assistant on farm', which he would eventually take over when his father died. There is no evidence that Bart English ever did military service. His parliamentary voting qualification in 1918 and 1919 was from residency at Moor Place Farm, and not from military service. It seems therefore that the person appearing before the tribunal on

3 May 1916 was B.W. English, and that there was a typographical error in the newspaper report. He successfully avoided conscription at a later appeal.

Lower down in the same article, the *Mercury* reported on another Yateley man: 'In the case of Charles Wheeler, farmer, of Yateley, the tribunal dismissed the appeal on the undertaking that the man would not be called up for a month.' Charles Wheeler was the 37-year-old unmarried son of George and Mercy Wheeler who farmed Dungell's Farm. When Charles had been baptized at St Peter's in 1878, his father was described as a pedlar. In 1882, when Charles was admitted to Yateley Village School, his father was described as a hawker. Most probably the family were settled gypsies. Charles Wheeler joined the 4th Battalion of the Hampshire Regiment. His father, George, was then 76 years old, and the tribunal left him to handle the farm by himself.

Dungell's Farm was one of Yateley's medieval farms. At the end of the nineteenth century, it was amalgamated into the large landholdings of the Kelsey family. During the war, the ancient building was occupied by George Wheeler as the Kelseys' tenant, living there with his wife, Mercy, and their family. After the war, the old building was demolished and the building in the picture was built. This new house was demolished after the Second World War to make way for new housing estates. (Jean McIlwaine)

It was a similar outcome in August for the farmer's son at Chandler's Farm, according to the *Reading Mercury* of 26 August 1916:

'Mr George Greaves appealed on behalf of his son, George Henry Greaves, aged 19, single. Mr Greaves rents Chandlers Farm (100 acres) at Yateley, and his son works for him as foreman and cowman. Mr Greaves also has a dairy shop in Camberley, which he attends to himself. – Appeal dismissed.'

CHANDLERS FARM, YATELEY, Hants.
and High Street, CAMBERLEY, Surrey,

....*192*.......

M..

Bot. of **G. GREAVES,**

Cowkeeper & Dairyman

Pure Milk.   Fresh Butter.   New Laid Eggs.

This is a counter cheque book receipt given by George Greaves of Chandlers Farm to his customers when they made a purchase from him. He had a shop in the High Street in Camberley before he established the dairy in Yateley. (Valerie Kerslake)

George Greaves of Camberley had purchased 58 acres of Chandlers Farm on 28 November 1913 from Frederick George Fullbrook, decorator, of Yateley. Fred Fullbrook had purchased the greater part of Chandlers and Mascall Farms from a Reading solicitor, Hubert May, in October 1910. These two farms covered much of the land immediately west of what we now call Chandlers Lane and immediately east of Mill Lane, plus much of the land between these two lanes.

These two ancient farms had been amassed into one large holding by Thomas 'shopkeeper' Bunch in the late eighteenth century, and then had been managed by his executors, the Ellis family, until the trust had gone bankrupt in the agricultural depression of the 1870s, when the wealthy Goddard family of Farnborough foreclosed on the mortgage.

Part of Hubert May's property holdings in Yateley had been purchased by Bertie A. Fullbrook. In March 1911, the latter had transferred ownership of part of his development land to Miss Annie Elizabeth English, the sister of Bart W. English who appeared at the 3 May 1916 conscription Appeal Tribunal. Neither Bart nor Annie ever married, and in later life they lived together in various houses around Yateley Green. Bertie Fullbrook married their sister, Alice May English, in 1908. One of Bertie's older brothers had already married one of Bart and Annie's older sisters in 1897. There were very close ties between the two families.

Bertie Alfred and Frederick George were brothers. Fred was the older by three years and had purchased the two farms from Hubert May as potential development land. They first built larger houses on the eastern side of Mill Lane. Bertie Fullbrook is listed in the *Kelly's Directories* of 1911 and 1912 as living in a large new house called Fir Glen, styling himself as 'builder'. By 1915, Colonel William Hill-Climo, a retired Indian Army surgeon, was in residence. Bertie had moved to Green Gables, another new house which he had built at the junction of Mill Lane and the road we now call Frys Lane. On the same block of land, Bertie developed Coronation Road, completing several houses before the demands of war dried up building materials and labour.

In the first decade of the twentieth century, Yateley's building stock had increased by about one third, and the population expanded by nearly 500. The number of new houses built between 1901 and 1911 was 145. Only twenty-two new houses were completed in the next decade, so it seems that in 1916 the good times were well past for Yateley's housing developers.

The two Fullbrook brothers appeared at the Appeal Tribunal in Basingstoke on the same day, according to the *Reading Mercury* of 14 October 1916:

'HAMPSHIRE APPEAL TRIBUNAL

A double sitting of Hampshire Appeal tribunal took place at Basingstoke ... Mr W H Myers presided in the Council Chamber, there being with him Sir C Brett, Mr G Dominey and Mr W J Willis. The cases dealt with here were from the Hartley Wintney, Fleet, Kingsclere, and Basingstoke rural districts.

'Mr E T Close appeared for Mr F G Fullbrooke, motor car proprietor of Yateley, against whose exemption the military authorities appealed. Mr Marley said Fullbrook had claimed that there was great necessity for his business, but he was away at Bexhill for a considerable time teaching a lady to drive a car, and the business was left to itself. Mr Fullbrook, in reply, said that the machinery for making shell caps had only been delivered on September 23rd, and he would now deliver about three dozen a week. He did the motor work for the Yateley Hospital, and did local repairs. – The tribunal dismissed the military appeal.

'The military authorities appealed the withdrawal of the conditional exemption granted to Mr B A Fullbrook of Yateley, wheelwright, for whom Mr E T Close appeared. For the military Mr Marley said that instead of wheelwright's work Mr Fullbrook had immediately undertaken a job of doing a house up. Mr Fullbrook said his business was wheelwrighting exclusively, and he put in a list of people in the neighbourhood for whom he had done work. - Military appeal dismissed.'

It seems that the Fullbrook brothers were ever resourceful and entrepreneurial: Fred had decided to go into the armaments business, albeit on a small scale, and Bertie had reverted to his original trade; both had other irons in the fire.

The next we hear of Fred Fullbrook is that he had joined up on 21 May 1917 as a motor driver with the Army Service Corps. In the meantime, something must have gone wrong with his scheme to produce shell caps in Yateley. He was discharged on 24 October 1917, having spent practically his whole time at the Connaught Hospital in Marlborough Lines in North Camp, Aldershot. The Connaught specialized in venereal diseases, but Fred was diagnosed as having neurasthenia, a nervous condition he had had since childhood. A Special Medical Board reviewed his case in London and approved his discharge as medically unfit. Fred's address given in his service papers was The Motor Garage, Yateley. When Bertie lived there with his family during the Second World War, this was called The Plough Garage.

The Plough Inn stood where the Co-op supermarket is now. James Hearmon had died at the age of 76 in 1909, but his wife, Margaret, and her family continued to run the pub during the First World War. Albert Thomas Hearmon was the licensed victualler when he was called up in 1916. The houses to the right of centre are recognisable today. (Richard Johnston)

Wartime Marriages In Yateley

There were twenty-six marriages at St Peter's Yateley during the First World War. Eleven of them recorded the groom's occupation as a serviceman. The first wartime wedding of a serviceman was on 30 April 1915. The groom was Alfred Walter Eckton, a sergeant in the Royal Field Artillery who had signed up as a Regular in 1902. His address on the marriage certificate states his residence was in Edinburgh, but he was born in Minstead in the New Forest. The bride was Edith Maud, daughter of William and Sarah Ann Backhurst of Globe Farm, Darby Green. Maud had a daughter, Dorothy Cecilia, born on 7 May 1916, baptized at St Peter's on 20 August.

Maud's father was the farm bailiff of Globe Farm, describing himself on her marriage certificate as a market gardener. By the end of the war, three of Maud's younger brothers and two of her brothers-in-law would be serving in the forces. One of her brothers, Herbert Backhurst, would be killed in France serving with the Hampshire Regiment. As a Regular, Alfred Eckton stayed with the Army after the end of the war, and Maud joined her husband in India in 1921.

The wedding in Yateley of an officer on leave hit the national newspapers, as the bride was the daughter of Sir Charles and Lady Stewart-Wilson. The marriage was a love match: the bride, Jean Blanche, and the groom had met in India when Sir Charles had been a senior member of the Indian Government; the groom, Captain John Archibald Ainslie, had been in India serving with his regiment, the King's Own Scottish Borderers. Sir Charles had forbidden the marriage in India until his daughter was of age. Captain Ainslie had secured leave from Egypt to enable him to wed his bride on Valentine's Day 1916. The groom's parents then lived in Tasmania, but were originally English. John Ainslie had been born in England and attended Brighton College.

Another 1916 wedding recorded in the newspapers was that of Grace Caroline Mary Davison of Newfield, one of the new houses owned by Hubert May, the Reading solicitor. Her house was just to the east of Fir Glen near the Mill Lane-Chandlers Lane junction. She and her widowed mother had moved into Newfield on 3 November 1913 from Ditchling, Sussex. The bride's father, John T. Davison, had been Chief Architect for the Royal Arsenal, Woolwich, during its massive expansion phase in the early twentieth century. Her new father-in-law was the Rev T.B. Watkins, the Rector of St James, Dover. He conducted the marriage service at St Peter's, assisted by his third son, the Rev C.S.T. Watkins, also of Dover, and by Yateley's curate, the Rev H.M.M. Piercy, who was himself just about to be called up into the Royal Army Medical Corps.

The groom was the Rev Wilfrid Egbert Watkins, Chaplain to the Forces at Shoreham Camp, opened in September 1914 to train many of the battalions of Kitchener's New Armies. By autumn 1915, the divisions making up Kitchener's New Army had been moved to France and, by the date of the wedding on 20 June 1916, Shoreham had become a rehabilitation centre for the wounded. One can imagine the need for the ministrations of the chaplain and his new wife from Yateley.

As 1916 drew to its close, Elizabeth Wheeler of Dungell's Farm, whose brother, Charles, had unsuccessfully appealed earlier in the year against conscription, married Arthur William Hilton at St Peter's on 16 December. Her new husband was another Regular soldier, and was not from the local Hilton family established for over a century in Yateley. He came from Hale Magna in Lincolnshire. The wedding took place while he was home on leave, serving in the 1st Battalion of The Rifle Brigade. His service number indicates he joined the regiment in 1905. The 1st Battalion took part in most of the main battles of the British Army during the First World War. On the first day of the Battle of the Somme, the battalion sustained a 62 per cent casualty rate. After the war, Arthur Hilton took over the running of Dungell's Farm.

CHAPTER 4

1917

Yateley Military Hospital

By the beginning of 1917, the Vicar of Yateley had made it known he intended to leave the parish. The ward of Yateley Military Hospital using the Vicarage therefore had to close on 25 January 1917, having treated 831 soldiers. The need for private houses in which the Red Cross volunteers could nurse the wounded back to health was as great as it had ever been. Consequently, fresh arrangements had to be made.

Before St Peter's Church was burnt down by an arsonist in 1979, it had retained its medieval character. The wooden rood screen was made by the Bunch brothers, still living on Vicarage Road during the First World War. The stained glass east windows above the altar by Burne-Jones were presented by the Stilwell family. The north wall on the left has Saxon origins. (Malcolm Miller)

This was not the only closure or the only resignation in the early months of 1917. The Yateley, Hawley, Minley & Eversley Cottage Hospital on Cricket Hill temporarily closed on 1 May owing to lack of funds. This was the local hospital for local people. In April, the Rector of Eversley, the Rev Mosley, announced he too was resigning. Both the Rector of Eversley and the Vicar of Yateley had taken a strong lead in their communities when war broke out in 1914. By the early months of 1917, many men who had been working in the two parishes had been conscripted. There were mounting casualty figures abroad, and at home escalating food prices and more atrocious weather. Those left in Yateley and Eversley must have wondered how they would continue to cope.

Miss Anne Tindal again stepped into the breach. The ward at Fir Grove was now separated from Yateley Hospital, renamed Eversley Military Hospital, and further expanded, even to the extent of having tented accommodation on the lawns. The ward which had operated in Yateley Vicarage was replaced immediately by moving it to Yateley Lodge, on the main road at the bottom of Cricket

More wounded soldiers arriving by ambulance from Aldershot. Firgrove Auxiliary Military Hospital started as a ward of the Yateley hospital at the Vicarage, but by 1917 Firgrove operated separately. Its capacity expanded throughout the war, all under the direction of Firgrove's owner, Miss Anne Tindal, assisted by the ladies of Red Cross Detachment Hants 94. (George Trevis)

Hill. Miss Constance Margaret Marx, who had volunteered for service in Serbia in 1915, went abroad again in November 1916 to Rumania, serving with the Scottish Women's Hospital. So Yateley Lodge stood empty. Although the Red Cross appears to have no records for the hospital, Mrs Sylvia Macrae's record shows she was appointed Assistant Commandant of Yateley Military Hospital in January 1917 and Miss Beatrice Stilwell continued in her position as Quartermaster.

Mrs Valerie Kerslake has collected oral history notes over many years. When she interviewed Mrs Fred Bunch of 5 Moulsham Copse Lane in July 1986, Mrs Bunch said she had:

> 'lived in this council house since it was built 60 years ago [so ca.1926]. Father returned from [blank] on ship with Sir [blank] & Lady Cope who asked him to work for them at Bramshill (gardener?) ... In [the] 1914 war [I] cooked at war hospital at "big white house with the big cedar in garden at bottom of road leading to the Flats". Then at Princess [ie

A group of the laundry staff working at Firgrove Military Hospital. Sarah Horne is standing with the basket. In 1914 she was a 54-year-old widow with three sons who became eligible for service during the war. Her second son, William, emigrated to Australia and joined the Australian Army, embarking with the 24th Infantry Battalion on 11 January 1916. (Horne family album)

Sarah Horne (with basket) at Fir Grove

Empress] Eugenie's hospital in Farnborough; cooked special food for officers having ops; they came down to thank her before they left. Lots of royalty about.'

Mrs Fred Bunch had been born Ada Dupree. Fred was the youngest of the ten children of Daniel and Emily Bunch, and therefore the youngest brother of Edwin and Samuel Bunch who had served with the Royal Engineers in Salonika. Ada had a younger sister, Lilian Dupree, who married Bertram Bunch in 1927. This Bertram Bunch is not to be confused with another son of Daniel and Emily Bunch, Bert Bunch, who emigrated to Canada but was killed on 15 August 1917 at Vimy Ridge, serving in the 48th Highlanders in the Canadian Army. He is inscribed on Yateley War Memorial as Herbert Bunch.

It is interesting to note that Miss Ada Dupree was only 19 when she was cooking at Yateley Lodge, and only 20 when she 'cooked special food for officers' at the Empress Eugenie's military hospital at Farnborough Hill. The minimum age to enrol as a VAD was

This postcard is the only image of wounded soldiers at Yateley Lodge after the military hospital transferred there in 1917. We have to rely on oral history from several sources for confirmation that Yateley Lodge served as a hospital. (Philip Todd)

then 23. There is no Red Cross record card for Ada Dupree, which emphasizes the value of oral history records.

Nurses Abroad

Miss Constance Margaret Marx was not the only Yateley lady who served abroad as a nurse. Miss Yvonne Fitzroy, the granddaughter of Lady Fitzroy of Frogmore, had volunteered as a VAD at a friend's house in Derbyshire. When in August 1916 Dr Elsie Inglis called for women to accompany her to Rumania to staff the Scottish Women's Hospital to nurse the wounded of the Serbian Army, Yvonne immediately volunteered. The Serbs had been driven out of their own country by the Austrians, but were now fighting with the Rumanians, who had declared war on the Central Powers on 27 August 1916. In January 1918, Miss Fitzroy published a book giving a very detailed account of her experiences. Starting with the voyage to Archangel accompanying the Serbian troops, her account ended with her return voyage in June 1917 from Bergen to Aberdeen and the words, 'Nothing will make me believe that Aberdeen is not the eighth wonder of the world and the the most beautiful city of earth.'

From Yvonne Fitzroy's letters and scrapbooks preserved in Edinburgh University Library, it seems she knew Dr Inglis' personal driver well. In a letter home, Yvonne referred to the chauffeur using a nickname her own family would also know. From this one reference, and her record with the Scottish Women's Hospital, it seems probable that the driver of Dr Inglis' car was Miss Margaret Marx. Miss Marx served in Rumania from 8 November 1916 to 1 August 1917.

Miss Vera Collum was trained to run the X-ray machine in the Scottish Women's Hospital at Royaumont in France. She wrote under a *nom de plume* for *Blackwood's Magazine*. One vivid article tells how she was nearly drowned when her cross-Channel ferry was torpedoed. She did not live in Yateley, but the Society acquired her personal papers from a relative who did live here.

Sister Patience Alice Stooks was gazetted on 4 January 1917 as 'mentioned in despatches' while serving in the Territorial Force

Nursing Service. The Rev Charles Stooks, Yateley's Vicar until 1905, had two daughters who served as nurses in France. At the outbreak of war, Patience was a nurse at Addenbrook Hospital. As a Territorial, she was immediately called-up and transferred to a war hospital at Trinity College, Cambridge, but was quickly moved to France, where she worked for the duration of the war.

Patience's younger sister, Phoebe Stooks, also worked in France, but as a volunteer with the Red Cross. Neither sister lived in Yateley during the First World War, but they had spent their childhood here. Their father and mother are buried in the churchyard alongside the imposing monument to their two brothers, one of whom died in the Great War. Second Lieutenant Herbert Drummond Sumner Stooks died of wounds inflicted while serving with the 52nd Company of the Machine Gun Corps in France. His brother, Major Charles Sumner Stooks, who served during the First World War in the 62nd Punjabis in Africa, came back to Yateley after the war and lived here throughout the Second World War. Phoebe also returned to Yateley to live at Jackanapes, one of the then separate houses now joined to create Forge Court and Sadlers Court, connecting them all in one long row to the White Lion.

Many people in Yateley will know Yateley Industries for the Disabled in its prominent position in the centre of the village, opposite Yateley Manor. Some will know that the workshops and special accommodation were founded by Miss Jessie Vera Lawford Brown. Few will know that she was Britain's first orthopaedic aftercare sister, working at Baschurch in Shropshire, where she had her initial training before the First World War. Even fewer will know that Jessie Brown served as a nurse on the Western Front in France from 1914-1917. The only record we have found is her obituary in *The Times* on 28 April 1983:

> *'In 1910 she started training with Sister (Dame) Agnes Hunt and soon became an expert orthopaedic nurse. After nursing soldiers in France, in 1917 she was put in charge of a group of clinics, and surprised the patients by arriving to visit them on a motorcycle. The surgeon, G R Girdlestone, invited her to join him in Oxford to set up similar clinics.'*

Appalling Weather

Meanwhile, William Burrows Tice, who ran the bakery and shop at Goose Green Cottage, and who had noted down the bad weather in his pocket book in 1916, continued to do so into 1917:

'November 4th, 1916: Fearful rough wet day. Glass at lowest point. Went over the mark and nearly at "set fair".

'January 1917: Most severe weather almost all the month and up till the 16th February [also] 20, 24, 28 and 30th. In some parts 26 deg of frost were registered. No such long spell since 1895. Skating everywhere.

'April 1917: Winter 1916-17 longest winter for 81 years. Snow fell in October and more or less each month till April. First spring day Primrose Day on April 19th.

'July 28th, 1917: began to rain and rained almost incessantly for a whole week to August 4th. Greatest rainfall ever registered for the time of year 4¼ inches in one week.'

A Photochrome postcard of a snowy scene looking across Yateley Green from near Old School Lane towards Brookfield and Brook Cottages. Brookfield is now listed Grade II. Regimental Quartermaster Sergeant Charles Henry Turrell was registered there as an absent voter in 1918 and 1919 during his war service in France. His wife and young children were probably living at Brookfield in the First World War as they were related to Charles Frederick Morgan, a draper, another tenant of Richard Kelsey who owned Brookfield. Turrell came from Bognor, but short-term arrangements were frequently made during the war to enable families to be near servicemen. (Jean McIlwaine)

The Death Toll Mounts

If the bad weather was depressing and inconvenient, the worsening news from the war fronts must have kept the villagers in a constant state of anxiety. Graham Fleuty, author of *Yateley Men at War – Heartbeats of Remembrance*, has written about 1917:

> 'Just imagine the horror of 1917 when a further 14 young men from Yateley died in just ten months. Many tears must have been shed at the Manor, Mill Lane, Up Green, Cricket Hill, Church Farm and Holly Hill Cottage.
>
> 'Tom Hicks and Edward Robertson died on the same day at Vimy Ridge. Bertie Bunch died four months later at Hill 70. Henry Cottrell and James Sillence were mown down on the same day after crossing the River Euphrates in an attempt to relieve the siege of Kut. Alf Blackman, Bertie Vokes, John Chute Ellis and Arthur Harrison died in Flanders during the Third Battle of Ypres. Robert Hoile, John Ainslie, Reginald Hicks and Herbert Stooks died in the Pas de Calais while William Abery was killed in northern Italy at Isonzo.
>
> 'Just imagine the anguish of loved ones missing and never found. Two of the above Yateley men are remembered on the Menin Gate, Ypres; and a further three on the Vimy Memorial.
>
> 'Just imagine the fear in the residents of Mill Lane where six of the families lost a son or father in four years of war. Which family would be next?
>
> 'We may never know the impact on Yateley people of these events and this terrible year of 1917.'

Graham describes those whose names were later recorded on the Yateley War Memorial – those with family connections in the Ecclesiastical Parish of St Peter's, which was mainly to the west of Cricket Hill, but included the old main road, which we now call Potley Hill, and parts of Darby Green.

The eastern part of Yateley Civil Parish was included in the ecclesiastical parish of Holy Trinity Hawley, which explains why some of the men from Yateley Civil Parish were recorded on the

pottery tiles on Hawley Memorial Hall. One of them, George
William Goddard of Starve Acre, was killed trying to relieve Kut
on 26 February 1917, the same day as Henry Cottrell and James
Sillence. Private Goddard was a member of the ubiquitous Goddard
family who had been in Yateley since the 1600s. His father and
grandfather were also named George. In 1861, grandfather Goddard
had been living in Yateley's Poor House after the inmates had been
moved to a new building in Farnborough. Private Goddard had three
siblings, his father had five and his grandfather eight siblings. News
of his death in Mesopotamia would have spread quickly around the
extended family in Yateley, Hawley and Cove.

Sapper George Cowie was a Glaswegian blacksmith who died
of a massive cerebral haemorrhage on 20 June 1917 in the 41st
Stationary Hospital in France. He was serving with F Cable Section
of the Royal Engineers. Perhaps the longest time he ever spent in
Yateley during the First World War was the month's leave from
10 January to 10 February 1917, visiting his wife, Edith May,
who was then living at Oak Cottage on Vicarage Road. She was
a daughter of William Bunch, one of the carpenter brothers who
ran their workshop a few doors along Vicarage Road nearer to the
vicarage. Sapper Cowie had married Edith May Bunch at St Peter's
Yateley on 30 September 1905. She gave birth to her second
daughter, Dorothy Edith, on 20 October 1917.

George Cowie had joined the Royal Engineers on 18 March
1904, initially in Chatham, but appears to have been transferred
quickly to the Royal Military College at Sandhurst, explaining how
a young man from Motherwell came to meet a Yateley girl. Their
first daughter, Agnes May Cowie, was baptized at St Peter's on
20 May 1906. George Cowie was voluntarily discharged on 26 June
1906 and joined the Army Reserve. The couple did not appear on
the Yateley census in 1911, but on 1 September 1915 Agnes was
enrolled at Yateley Village School, her former school being given as
Glasgow. Her parents' address was now The Green, Yateley. Edith
May Cowie, with her daughter, Agnes, had clearly decided to come
down from Glasgow to Yateley to live in one of the Bunch-owned
houses in Vicarage Road whilst her husband was serving abroad.

Edith May Cowie was still living in Yateley in 1920, because Agnes left the village school aged 14 on 16 April 1920, just days from the date of the consecration of the Yateley War Memorial. Edith May seems to have decided not to have her husband's name listed on the memorial. She did, however, add a personal memorial to him on her father's gravestone in the churchyard: 'Sapper George Cowie Royal Engineers, the beloved husband of May Bunch, who died at the 41st Stationary Hospital, Gailly, France, June 20th 1917, aged 33. His duty done.'

Another man whose total stay in Yateley was a few brief days was John Archibald Ainslie. Unlike George Cowie, the name John Ainslie was recorded on the Yateley War Memorial in 1920, even though his wife and her family had left Yateley some two years earlier. Although Captain Ainslie was born in England, attended Brighton College and joined a Scottish regiment, in 1920 his parents were living in Tasmania. He only set foot in Yateley for his wedding on St Valentine's Day 1916 to Jean Blanche Stewart-Wilson, the daughter of Sir Charles and Lady Stewart Wilson of the Manor House. The Society's archive has handwritten notes written by Sam Chesterman (b. 1900):

When in the Edwardian and Delhi Durbar carefree days, and the British Raj life was still in its hey days, it was said a young lieutenant and the young daughter of Sir Charles and Lady Stewart Wilson fell in love with each other. Sir Charles held an important position in the Bombay Presidency and the parents thought their daughter too young but said, if the lovers were of the same mind after a certain period has passed, permission would be given.

When the period had passed the family had taken residence at Yateley Manor House, also the First World War had begun. As the lovers were of the same mind they were married, but soon after the young officer died in the war and the young bride was inconsolable.

On his belongings sent home from the war, often with the filth and gore of the trenches, the young lady took them up to her bedroom and shut the door. After some time had passed the parents became worried and opened the door.

She was asleep with her arms clasped round his army great coat. She was carrying his child, I believe. On Yateley War Memorial is his name, Capt Ainsley [sic].

Sam Chesterman did not note his source, but it seems from the continuation of his notes about the Stewart-Wilsons that his information could have come from a parlour maid named Hetty Cumnor.

Henry James Claridge is not recorded on the Yateley memorial, even though his step-mother was living in the family house on Vigo Lane when he was killed, and was still there in 1920. His father had died in 1914. Harry had joined the Army Service Corps as a Regular in 1908, but he was serving in the Royal Garrison Artillery when he was killed in Flanders on 29 September 1917. He was from the family of seven children of Thomas and Lucy Claridge living on Rigby's Lane, Cricket Hill, in 1901. Born on 1 December 1889, Harry had been enrolled at Yateley's village school on the Green at the age of 3. When he left school, he had been apprenticed to Harry Tyler as a baker and, when war was declared, was working as a baker in West Ealing, living with his eldest brother, William, and William's wife, Miriam.

Village School Football Team
The Society has two picture postcards of pre-war village school football teams. One card is dated 1908 and the other is undated, but the postmark is 1914. The postmarked card has a note attached apparently giving the names of eleven of the thirteen boys in the picture. It seems likely that the list of names attached to the card postmarked 1914 actually applies to the 1908 postcard, because all the boys named had left the school aged 14 between 1910 and 1913, and one had left the village in 1911. Nothing is more poignant than looking into the faces of the young footballers knowing that at least three of them would meet their deaths in the war.

The boys named on the note were born between 1896 and 1899. The older boys were eligible to volunteer at the outbreak of war,

*This photograph of the 1908 school football team includes the Matthews brothers.
(Jean McIlwaine)*

and the younger ones were required to register under the Derby
Scheme. We know from Dougie Gibbs, a later headmaster's son
who attended the school in the 1920s, that there were four classes
covering the age range of 3 to 14. The boys in the football team
were probably in the same class in 1908. These footballers at the
village school represent all Yateley boys who made up the rank
and file of the armed forces in the First World War. It was a rare
occurrence for a boy from the village school to become an officer.
Yateley boys who made up the officer class had been sent away to
the major public schools.

One of the young lads pictured on the 1908 postcard was Charles
Francis Matthews (b. 27 February 1897), who was killed on 8 May
1917 serving with the 1st Battalion, East Surrey Regiment. In
1911, he lived with his family in Castle Bottom. The eldest of the
boys named in the football group was Charlie's elder brother, Harry

Matthews (b. 19 January 1896). His service number indicates that he had joined the East Surrey Regiment early in the war. He was killed in France on 23 August 1918, having transferred to the Machine Gun Corps. The tragedy for this family did not end there. Having lost both her children, Mrs Sarah Ann Matthews herself died of cardiac failure in October 1918, shortly after Harry was killed. Although these two brothers went to school in Yateley, they lived in Eversley. Their names are inscribed on the Eversley War Memorial.

The third member of the 1908 football team to die was Charles Albert Butler, who had been able to enjoy the bell-ringing excursion to Amesbury church whilst the 4th Hants were training on Salisbury Plain in 1914. Unlike most of his comrades, he did not immediately sign the Territorial Force 'Imperial Service Obligation', agreeing to serve abroad. On 8 March 1916, when he was serving on the home front with the 84th Provisional Battalion of the Hampshire Territorials, he did signed the Obligation. The alternative would have been conscription. He was transferred to the 2/8th Battalion of the Warwickshire Regiment in May 1916, rose to the rank of lance sergeant and was killed in Belgium in April 1918. Charlie Butler was one of twenty-three members of the 8th Odiham Boy Scouts who had served in the First World War.

8th Odiham (Yateley) Boy Scouts

Yateley's earliest Scout troop had been formed on 5 October 1911, only two years after the scouting movement itself. They were based at the scout hut on Firgrove Road. The modern building is called the Macrae Hut after Miss Dorothy Macrae, the daughter of Mrs Sylvia Macrae of Kerala. Miss Macrae had taken over as Scoutmaster in November 1915 after the two male Scouters were called up. Village schoolmaster John Carter had already become Assistant Scoutmaster, adding to the many roles he had during the war.

Five former members of the 8th Odihams were killed during the war and six more were wounded. Percy Alderman, a former patrol seconder, had been killed in 1916, followed by James Sillence in February 1917. Wilfred James Maybanks had been

A postcard entitled 'Yateley Scouts at Work'. The Scouts were tasked with helping the war effort from its outset. During the early months they could even be assigned to defend strategic points. During the war they were given rifle training at the Yateley small-bore rifle range. (Malcolm Miller)

the Patrol Leader of the Curlews throughout the war. The troop still possesses the attendance register showing that Wilfred barely missed any meetings. His very last attendance was on 31 October 1917. On 11 November 1917 he was 18 years old and eligible for war service. His father had died in December the previous year and his 15-year-old brother, Ernest William, would die on 18 November. Wilfred himself could not have been a very tough child, as his parents sent him away to 'The General or Royal Mineral Water Hospital' on Upper Borough Walls, Bath. As an 11-year-old, he was recorded in the 1911 census as a patient at the hospital. There were 149 patients in twenty-four night wards, looked after by twelve nurses and eleven servants. It is not known why he was there, and how he was financed given that his father was Yateley's 'carrier', running a service to Reading. What did his mother think as she kissed him goodbye to leave for the war front? Wilfred Maybanks was killed a month before his 19th birthday while serving in France with the 1/7th Battalion of the West Yorkshire Regiment.

A high turnover in Yateley Village School

Headmaster John Carter and his small team of teachers had to cope with the large turnover in the school. Graham Sargent has analyzed the school admissions registers:

Year	Admissions			Leavers	Change
	Jan-Jul	Aug-Dec	Annual	Annual*	Annual*
1911	15	6	21		
1912	19	9	28		
1913	16	11	27		
1914	31	10	41	4	+37
1915	56	23	79	49	+30
1916	24	30	54	52	+2
1917	30	18	48	42	+6
1918	35	22	57	53	+4
Totals			279	200	79

Note: * No information available for blank years

For a school with a maximum capacity of 180 children, the turnover during the four years of the war is rather large. There were several reasons why a child might leave a school during the First World War, the main one being that they had reached their 14th birthday. It would be expected that a school of 180 pupils operating at capacity would, on average, have eighteen pupils reaching 14 years of age in each year. So what factors could have caused the excess withdrawals over eighteen?

To produce an average eighteen withdrawals each calendar year at age 14, admissions must also average eighteen per year. During the First World War, the admissions averaged nearly fifty per year, producing a rising annual increase in pupil numbers. The large number of admissions and withdrawals during the war is a manifestation of the comings and goings of families in the village. In each year there were significant numbers of children who were taught at the school for less than one year, sometimes for just a few days. The reasons for these temporary stays are different in almost every case.

Yateley Village School seen across the playground. The headmaster, Mr John Carter, is seen in the picture. The house in which he lived with his family is on the right. John Carter organized the national egg collection in Yateley, was Assistant Scoutmaster and was the commanding officer of the Yateley company of the volunteeer battalion of the Hampshire Regiment when it was formed in 1916. (Jean McIlwaine)

On 13 October 1915, three daughters of Frederick Cumner were withdrawn from the school after spending only twenty-three days there. Exactly a year earlier, Albert George Cumner, a son of Frederick Charles and Harriett Cumner, had been baptized at St Peter's. The baptismal register gave their address as 23 Porteus Road, Paddington, and Charlie's occupation as Royal Field Artillery. When he had married Harriett Davis, a Yateley girl, at St Peter's on 16 October 1905, he was a 'sergeant in the RFA' and gave his address as Newbridge, County Kildare. However, he was born in Camberley and his parents lived in Sandhurst. He is one of the few men with a Yateley connection recorded in the National Roll of the Great War: '*He was sent to France* [14 Mar] *in 1915 and took part in the heavy fighting at Festubert and Loos* [as a battery sergeant major].' The reason his daughters spent three weeks at school in Yateley was because he had four weeks' leave after returning home from France on 14 September 1915, and Fred's family came to stay with his wife's parents in Yateley.

Commanded by John Carter the schoolmaster, the Yateley platoon of the 1st Hampshire Volunteer Regiment was 13th Platoon in D Company, formed in 1916. Most of the men were beyond the age at which they would otherwise have been conscripted. Some of the Yateley platoon lived in Eversley, which never managed to form its own company. (Malcolm Miller)

Two years later, in July 1917, two of the Cumner girls, Millicent and Winifred, were back at Yateley village school, but this time they stayed for 120 days in Yateley over the summer holiday, not returning to London until the end of October. This was at the time of the first Gotha bomber raids on London, so perhaps they had been sent to Yateley for safety.

By the end of September 1917, the Gothas had been joined by the four-engine bomber, the Zeppelin-Staaken RA501, nicknamed the 'Giant'. The population of London was thoroughly alarmed by the intensity of night-time air raids. An estimated 300,000 people were sheltering in Underground stations and others were leaving London. On 6 October, the *Camberley News* reported that large influxes of women and children had been arriving from London by train:

'The rush commenced on Friday [28 September 2017] and Saturday, and on Sunday and Monday they were arriving by practically every train. The women, almost without exception, in seeking apartments, made no secret of the fact

This certificate was proudly shown to us by the late Geoff Bunch who lived in one of the 'Bunch houses' on Vicarage Road until his death. As his father William George Bunch was over the age to be conscripted in 1916, he volunteered for the Yateley company of the newly formed 1st Volunteer Battalion of the Hampshire Regiment the First World War equivalent of the Home Guard. (Yateley Society Archive)

that they were unable to any longer endure the nerve-strain occasioned by the raids. It may be a matter of wonder to many people who do not know why there should have been such a rush in this district, but the explanation is very simple. Many battalions of the London Regiment have been training in the neighbourhood, and while the men were at the camp their female relatives have visited the district in hundreds, in the majority of cases stopping over the weekend.

'The men to a great extent are now serving overseas, and leaving London, the women with their children, having nowhere else to go, have come to the neighbourhood in the hope of being put up in places where they formerly lodged. But in a very great number of cases they have been disappointed for the reason that their former lodgings are now occupied by the relatives of men still in training [at] *the camp.'*

Yateley's Gypsies

For many years, the village headmaster and his staff had had considerable experience of teaching children for very short periods. For decades, Romany children had been taught at the school when their parents' caravans and tents were parked on Yateley Common. The gypsies would arrive in Yateley during the winter months. For example, during the winter of 1903 to 1904, twenty gypsy children were admitted as pupils between October and February, with eleven of them arriving in January 1904. They were from the Smith, Green, Gregory, Blake, Hicks, Harrison and Ayres families. The occupation of the 'parent or guardian' in the admissions registers was noted as 'gypsy', and the address 'Yateley Common'.

Gypsy families had camped on Yateley Common on their travels since the seventeenth century or before. Starting in 1861, some families were recorded in the census, stating whether they lived in a tent or a caravan. In the 1891 Yateley census, there were eight families living in tents, but only one, the family of Thomas and Britannia Gregory, living in a caravan. Gypsy children had attended the Yateley National C of E School sporadically since it was founded in 1865. By the turn of the century, some gypsy

The main trunk road to the west of England (now the A30) crossed Yateley Common. The common had been a military training area for Sandhurst cadets for most of the nineteenth century. During the Great War, it was a training area under Aldershot Command. Aptly named Hartfordbridge Flats, it was ideal open country to practise trench warfare. (Jean McIlwaine)

families were starting to settle permanently in Yateley, whilst others still preferred the life of a traveller.

Henry Hicks had married Christabel James on 1 January 1889 at St Mary's Eversley. The marriage certificate gave their address as The Flats, Eversley. Henry was the son of Sylvanus Hicks and Mary Williams, and Christabel was the daughter of Alfred James and Sophia Gregory. Christabel baptized ten children at St Peter's Yateley between 1894 and 1911. The 1911 census shows she gave birth to a total of thirteen children, only seven of whom were still living in 1911. Of those, John Hicks, aged 23, was the oldest. His only surviving brother was Henry Hicks, aged 21. Christabel's surviving daughters were Mary, Aggie, Victoria, Phoebe and Sophia.

Henry and Christabel were living in a tent on Yateley Common in April 1891, but by the time of the assessments for 1910 Land Tax – Lloyd George's 'Domesday' – they appeared to be living in a small thatched cottage surrounded by Yateley Common, situated more or less where the eastern end of the RAF Hartfordbridge runway was built during the Second World War.

Their eldest son, John Hicks, died of wounds near Cambrai in France on 11 February 1918. He was serving with the 6th Battalion, Somerset Light Infantry. John Hicks was not the only person with Romany heritage to be killed during the war: at least four others were killed, and many others served valiantly. Servicemen from gypsy families are particularly hard to trace in the military records. Many had very common names, and some men retained their mother's surname. Leonard Lee, for example, of Sandpit Cottage, Yateley Common, was the son of Charles Doe and Cinderella Lee. Gypsy families can be spotted in census records because very often each child in the family had a different birthplace. But often those children could have been baptized elsewhere, registered in a completely different district, perhaps not registered at all. Some gypsy children were baptized very many times to take advantage of the church's missionary zeal, which sometimes included financial benefits.

Gypsy men from Yateley fought hard, and at least one, Edward Earle Coles of Starve Acre, was awarded the Military Medal. He enlisted with the 1st Battalion, Berkshire Regiment on 13 August 1914 and had already received a wound to his foot which required him to be sent back to England on 27 September 1914. He went back to the front. The award of his Military Medal appeared in the *London Gazette* on 11 February 1919. By then he had transferred to the 2nd Battalion. Edward Coles was only 20 when he joined up, and 27 when he died of pneumonia brought on by influenza in January 1922.

Like many young men returning from the war front, he had got married. His wedding to Florence Mary Martin at his parish church, Holy Trinity Hawley, was only six months before his death. Edward Coles had been born at Starve Acre, and both bride and groom gave their address as Blackwater. His father's name had been missing from his birth certificate, but it was given on the marriage certificate as George Voller, deceased.

Other members of the gypsy community are recorded elsewhere in this book.

Boundary House in Blackwater was Joby James' business premises during the First World War. In 1939 he was living at Oakleigh in Rosemary Lane, giving his occupation as 'Haulage and Government Contractor'. Born into a gypsy family on 21 November 1869, he is first recorded in the 1871 census living with six siblings in his father's caravan on Yateley Common. (Yvonne Allen)

Joby James' lorry in this postcard is quite probably the one he used to transport gravel from the pit in Darby Green to help construct the runways at Farnborough. (Malcolm Miller)

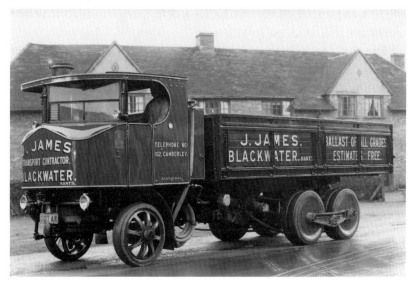

Cecilia's Story

The saddest story is of a young mother who, by November 1916, had had two infant daughters by her first husband, and was then pregnant with a son by her second husband. Cecilia Agar had married Arthur George Mustow in 1910. He was the son of the butler at Hawley Hill House; she was the daughter of Charles and Eliza Agar, born in a cottage on that part of Hartford Bridge Flats which was in the parish of Elvetham. After Cecilia and Arthur married, they lived in two rooms in a five-room house on London Road in Blackwater. They had two daughters: Florence and Ellen.

Arthur George Mustow worked as a carman on the railways in 1911, but his service number with the 1st Battalion of the Hampshire Regiment (6307) indicates that before 1911 he had already served as a Regular in the regiment. He was therefore called back as a reservist when war was declared. There are two pieces of evidence supporting this. He was named in the Roll of Honour published by the *Hants & Berks Gazette* listing all those Yateley men already serving in December 1914. Although his own service papers have not survived, service papers giving enlistment dates of soldiers in the Hampshire Regiment having numbers 6300 and 6310 have survived, their original enlistment dates being 2 March and 27 September 1901 respectively. Arthur Mustow therefore must have joined up originally in 1901.

The two service numbers immediately following that of Arthur Mustow are for John Edgell (6308) and Arthur George Howse (6309). All three of these men were living very close to each other in Hawley at the time they enlisted, all having lived at some time in Yateley. All three were killed in France between December 1914 and June 1915.

Cecilia Mustow's husband was the last to die, on 2 June 1915. Shortly after losing her husband, Cecilia also lost her youngest daughter. Ellen Gladys Mustow, only 18 months old, died of 'eclampsia and dentition' on 29 August 1915. The manner of her daughter's death must have been doubly distressing to Cecilia so soon after the death of her husband. There is no home address given on Arthur Mustow's Commonwealth War Graves Commission record, but the address on baby Ellen's death certificate is Darby Green. Cecilia may have been living with her brother-in-law and his wife at Frogmore Cottage.

It is perhaps not surprising that just three-and-a-half months after the death of her youngest daughter, and six-and-a-half months after the death of her first husband, Cecilia chose to marry again. Her second husband was Herbert Clifford Larder, a 28-year-old private from Mark in Somerset serving with the Royal Army Veterinary Corps. He had enlisted as a volunteer on almost the same day as Cecilia's first husband had been killed. Cecilia's second wedding was in St Peter's Church, Yateley, on 15 December 1915. The bride's sister, Florence, was one witness, and Lewis Pool, who lived in the Crescent in Darby Green, was the other. Both the bride and groom gave their address as Darby Green.

Cecilia's son, named exactly as his father, Herbert Clifford Larder, was born on 29 December 1917. The father's occupation was given as sergeant in the Army Veterinary Corps, with the address being Darby Green, Yateley. What the birth certificate did not state was that the baby's father had been dead for three months: Bert Larder had died in hospital in France on 12 September 1917.

The certificate for Cecilia's third marriage, to Christopher Byrne, a widower born in Dublin, shows her living at 7 Denmark Street, Aldershot, in October 1920. It is therefore not very likely that Cecilia was still living in Darby Green in April 1920 when the Yateley War Memorial was consecrated, and she became the only Yateley woman to have the names of two husbands recorded on it. If she did not personally supply the names of her two husbands to be recorded, that might account for the error in inscribing Bert Larder's name as 'Arthur Larder'.

Food Shortages

On 1 February 1917, Germany declared unrestricted submarine warfare on ships of any nation transporting cargoes to Britain. The USA broke off diplomatic relations with Germany two days later and declared war on 6 April 1917. Food shortages mounted in Britain as German submarines sank more and more thousands of tons of British and neutral nations' ships. The growing number of American troops arriving in England also had to be fed from the total foodstuff supplies in Britain.

The 24 March edition of the *Camberley News* announced that very few potatoes had arrived at Covent Garden that week. The newspaper reported that:

> '*Driven to distraction by the shortage, several retailers would willingly pay more than the price allowed by law to get supplies, and therefore pacify their customers, but wholesalers dare not fall in with illicit suggestions ... English potatoes and English swedes must not be sold at more that 1½d per lb.*'

The *Camberley News* had been reduced to four pages due to paper shortages, but devoted practically the whole of its front page to advice to local allotment holders and gardeners. The 7 July edition published a detailed list of all the Food Regulations then in force which specifically applied to the general public. As well as price controls to ration food supplies, government advertising during 1917 encouraged the idea of voluntary rationing, but eventually ration books had to be introduced in London on 25 February 1918, and nationwide by that summer.

Yateley people perhaps suffered less than those in towns and cities during the national food crisis. There were a large number of existing allotments in Yateley on two sites established well before the war. The Small Holdings and Allotments Act (1908) obliged local authorities to provide land for allotments, but the Rural District Council did not own Yateley's allotments. There were 6 acres of allotment gardens north of the green on Cricket Hill, capable of providing ninety-six standard allotments. To the west of Mill Lane, the even larger allotment gardens could provide 168 standard allotments. A standard allotment was 10 square poles (also known as square rods or perches), units of measurement dating back to Saxon times. Yateley's 264 standard allotments were sufficient to serve about 60 per cent of households in the entire civil parish, including farms, mansion houses and those houses already having large gardens.

Both allotment gardens were on land which had been part of the Manor of Hall Place. The three Mason sisters, who had inherited the manor and still lived at The Croft, owned the larger allotment gardens behind their house, west of Mill Lane. On the Tithe Map of 1844, this field was named Silk Croft because Captain George Mason had planted it out with mulberry trees to feed his silk worms. He had exhibited the woven silk at the Great Exhibition of 1851. J.P. Stilwell now owned the land at Cricket Hill after the break-up of the manor. On the Tithe Map, the site of this allotment garden was called Upper Common Field, part of the medieval common field system. Valerie Kerslake interviewed the late William Ernest (Bill) Liddiard (1903-1987) on 15 April 1986:

> *'Home was one of four small cottages on the north edge of the common at Cricket Hill, facing the old Cricketers. It would have been like many other cottages: a pump outside near the back door, perhaps shared with the next door household. An outside earth closet would be emptied from time to time and spread as fertiliser on garden or farmland. The kitchen had a bread oven and heavy iron hooks for hanging joints of bacon on, for his family, like many others, kept a pig. Usually it was sold to the butcher in the end.'*

The allotments were just to the north of the Liddiards' garden: 'Everyone expected to grow their own fruit and vegetables, and on some allotments there were chickens or beehives.' Bill remembered that George Ives, the publican of the Cricketers, kept chickens and let them free-range over the green. There were also many goats on Cricket Hill during the war.

When Bill was 12, he was offered a job as errand boy by the Oakshotts, who lived at the White House, which was,

> *'the grandest of the five large houses on the Green to the west of the White Lion. Bill would receive ten shillings*

A view of Cricket Hill House (now the Casa dei Cesari Hotel) from a position near the bottom of Tudor Drive looking across the stream which runs down Royal Oak Valley. Miss Mary Isabel Marson was living there on her own means in 1915. Still living there in 1939, she was the daughter of Frederick Boyd Marson of Highfield Park, Heckfield, a director of insurance companies who left £107,137 in his will, proved in 1910. (Jean McIlwaine)

and sixpence a week, twelve and six after two years. An errand boy's bike went with the job but no meals. When food began to be scarce in 1917 Bill would be required to bicycle to Yorktown each Monday to collect the butter and tea from the Home & Colonial, and he would also cash £25 for Dr Oakshott at Barclays Bank on the corner nearby. Sometimes he was sent to buy bread from the stores beside the church in Yateley and the manager, Mr E C Webley, might offer him a piece of cheese and a biscuit for his lunch but he always took it home.'

From the start of the war, local people had been used to giving produce from their gardens and allotments to support the local military hospitals. Sydney Loader recalls in his memoirs that he delivered produce from Mrs Masterman's garden at Heathcroft, where his father was gardener:

'The local gentry who still had large gardens and mostly had a gardener, supplied much of the vegetables, fruit, etc. Mrs Masterman sent to the Yateley Lodge Hospital, and I had to go down there with them on Saturday mornings. I saw the soldiers sitting out in the grounds in nice weather, dressed in light blue uniforms with red ties. Some were in wheel chairs some on crutches. I remember one man beautifully embroidering a table cloth with red fuchsias.'

The Yateley Military Hospital at Yateley Lodge closed for good in December 1917, four months after Miss Marx had returned from Rumania.

CHAPTER 5

1918

The Bishop of Winchester's New Year message was published in the *Eversley Parish Magazine*. He opened by predicting that 'It must be a sad year, it must carry an almost overpowering burden of anxiety and suspense.' But it was the opening paragraph of his letter for the following month, at the beginning of Lent, which best sums up the prevailing mood:

> '*My Dear people, it is not a time, as it seems to me, for saying much. It is the critical stage of the war. We hold our breath in suspense. We are awaiting the most colossal onslaught ever delivered. Can we under God withstand it, as our soldiers quietly and firmly believe? Can we at home hold on steadily without weakness and division among ourselves?*'

By the beginning of the year, the new Vicar of Yateley had been installed and was living at the vicarage. Eversley too had its new Rector, the Rev Maurice Tanner. He had been a housemaster at Cheltenham, but both he and his wife had strong family connections locally, reaching to Finchampstead and Yateley. Maurice Tanner was the nephew of Lady Glass, who had lived at Warbrook, Eversley, for over forty years. His brother was Brigadier General John Arthur Tanner, who had been killed at Arras on 23 July 1917. A year before he was killed, General Tanner had married Gladys Helen, the daughter of C.T. Murdoch MP JP of Buckhurst Park,

Wokingham. In 1921, the Rev Tanner's widowed sister-in-law, Gladys, remarried to Major General Sir William Andrew Liddell, becoming Lady Liddell of the Manor House, Finchampstead. Sir William had been Deputy Engineer-in-Chief of the British Expeditionary Force in 1916.

The Rev Tanner's wife also had strong local connections. One of them was Miss Currie, who lived in Up Green with Mrs Verini, who organized the entertainment for the wounded soldiers at Firgrove Military Hospital.

The Rev Arthur James Howell MA was installed at St Peter's on 25 July 1917, having arrived from Capel in Surrey. His family consisted of his wife, Lydia May, and his niece, Sybil, then aged 27. Sybil had been born Sybil Ione Moody in Braishfield on 23 November 1890. Her father, a magazine writer, was the Rev Howell's brother-in-law. By 1911, Sybil's surname had changed to Howell. She continued to live with the Vicar until he died.

Sybil had served for six weeks as a VAD at Netley Hospital in early 1917 before she came to Yateley. Her diary for 1918 details her work at Firgrove Hospital massaging patients. On 3 January she noted: 'Very cold, tried to snow. Busy massaging 10 patients. New boy Varley. 5 electrical cases.' On the following day she wrote, 'Coldest day we've had. Massaged morning and afternoon in cold room', and then on the 5th, 'Wee bit warmer. 10 patients to massage. Had to use my own Vim most of the time as the electric battery was broken.' On Tuesday 22 January she added:

> 'Miss Tindall motored me into Aldershot. Called at Headquarters, the Cambridge Hospital, and then Army & Navy Stores about supplies of food for the Hospital. Left my Electrical Machine at Hospital to be repaired.'

Treating the wounded with electrical therapy and massage had been introduced in 1914 in various military hospitals, including Netley and Aldershot. Minley Hospital had a special department, and it seems that Miss Tindal had introduced it at Firgrove.

Bad Weather and Bad News

Sybil Howell's diary entries in January 1918 almost invariably started with a mention of the bad weather: 'Woke up and found the world white so stayed in at home.' She also commented that food shortages were worsening. Because of these shortages, the government introduced midday meals at state schools. In Yateley, these meals were prepared in the parish room, a hut in the gardens of the Vicarage. On Monday 14 January, the day Sybil stayed at home because of the snow, she wrote in her diary: 'Helped at the school kitchen to feed 78 bears – they all got a steaming hot meal for 2d – bless 'em. I sampled the pudden jolly good.'

News from France in the spring of 1918 was very bad. Four men named on the Yateley War memorial were killed in March on four consecutive days. On 21 March, the German army launched their Spring Offensive, predicted in the Bishop of Winchester's pastoral letter as 'the most colossal onslaught ever delivered'.

On 22 March 1918, Lieutenant John Iltid Royds was the first man killed. He had lived with his parents at Brize Park, a large estate near Brentwood in Essex. Distantly related to the spinster Mason sisters, the daughters of Captain George Mason who had formed the Yateley Volunteers, John Royds was also distantly related to the Chairman of Yateley Parish Council, Mr A.H. Templer. His closest relation living in Yateley was his aunt, Miss Mary Alethea Mason, who lived at Aldenham on Yateley Green.

The last of the Yateley men to die was Private Clarence John Legg. He died of his wounds on 24 March, having served with the 1st Battalion, the Duke of Edinburgh's Wiltshire Regiment. His parents lived in Mill Lane, where his father had worked as a blacksmith before the war. Clarence Legg's mother, Laura, had already lost her only other son, Reggie Legg, at the Battle of Jutland. Her 51-year-old husband was also away serving as a shoeing smith in the Army Veterinary Corps.

The other two of the four men killed in the first days of the German Spring Offensive, George and Henry Harris, were first cousins. Their paternal grandparents were James and Sarah Harris, who were recorded in the 1871 census as living in a tent on Yateley

Common, together with William, Samuel and five younger children. William was the father of George Harris, killed on 23 March, and Samuel was the father of Henry Harris, killed on the 24th.

Not only were George and Henry's fathers brothers, born one year apart, their mothers were sisters too. Both sets of parents had married in 1877 at St Peter's. George's father, William, had married Elizabeth Grainger, and Samuel had married her sister, Deanah. The 1871 census records that Elizabeth and Deanah were living in Yateley Poor House, now demolished but on the site we now know as Silver Fox Farm. The Poor House, built centuries before on the western edge of Yateley Common, had long been redundant for its original purpose and had been sold in 1848 to another member of the Harris family. Elizabeth and Deanah's parents were James and Sophia Grainger. In 1871, James Grainger had been described as a pedlar and James Harris as a tinker.

By 1918, all these families had settled in local houses and all had acquired the parliamentary vote as a result of the Representation of the People Act 1918. George Harris' parents, William and Deanah, still lived in the Poor House in 1918, which had been renamed

Until the Second World War aerodrome was built in 1942, Vigo Lane ran north-south across the open and treeless Yateley Common from the Anchor pub to the right-angle bend near the modern gypsy camp on the road to Fleet. When the new Minley Auxiliary Military Hosptial at Minley Lodge needed to install a telephone, the line had to be run across the common from the Anchor. (Jean McIlwaine)

The Row. Henry Harris' parents, Samuel and Diana, lived at Heatherside View in Vigo Lane.

After George had married Mary Vickery at St Peter's in 1910, they lived at Monteagle Cottages. These were two semi-detached farm cottages owned by Monteagle Farm and facing onto the part of the common we now know as Blackbushe Airport. They were pulled down when RAF Hartfordbridge was built in 1942. George and Mary baptized four children, including Bertie Ploeg Harris, on 13 May 1917. The two eldest boys were George William (b. 6 November 1910) and William Albert (b. 17 August 1913). They were both enrolled at the village school in 1918 after their father had been killed.

At least five names of men with Romany ethnicity were inscribed on Yateley War Memorial in 1920, amounting to 12 per cent of the total. This is far higher than the proportion of persons with Romany ethnicity living in Yateley at the time.

Walking through Darby Green and Frogmore
The Battle of Amiens on 8 August 1918 is generally agreed to be when the tide of battle turned in favour of the Allies. The clock started ticking on the period of the Great War which has become known as 'the 100 days', ending on Armistice Day. Battle-ready American troops were arriving at the front in their hundreds of thousands. In January 1918, they held only 10km of the front; by 10 August, they held 126km of front, compared with the 150km still held by the British and 447km by the French. The weight of numbers of Allied servicemen, and their growing superiority in equipment and munitions, speeded the end of the war on the Western Front.

The final day for registration to vote in the 1918 parliamentary election was Monday 15 July 1918, twenty-five days earlier than the Battle of Amiens. The Representation of the People Act 1918 gave the vote to all men who served in the war, and women aged 28 and over. A feeling of hope was in the air, but there was still a tension. There was now constant movement of people and families in the village, particularly east of Cricket Hill.

What would have been your impressions on 15 July if you had walked along the main road from Yateley Lodge, at the bottom of

Cricket Hill, to reach the London road in Blackwater? You would have seen the character of the parish change as you reached Darby Green, and again as you walked on through Frogmore Green.

POTLEY HILL

The old main road we now call Potley Hill was dominated on its south side by Hilfield, the mansion house of the Stilwell family, who have played such a prominent part in our story. John Pakenham Stilwell, the retired banker and Navy Agent, was 85 years old. His wife, Georgina née Stevens, had died in 1916, but his daughters, Nora, Ethel and Beatrice, were still at home, the latter two now relieved of their VAD duties. Their sister, Alice, had resigned from Firgrove Hospital in March 1917 having completed 5,184 hours of nursing and massage since September 1914.

This view of Hilfield from the air was probably taken by Christopher Stilwell, a serving RAF officer in both wars. Son of Holt Stilwell and Elizabeth (Betty) Tindal, he was the younger brother of Jack Stilwell, who was wounded in Mesopotamia and became a PoW in Turkey. This view gives a good idea of the rural isolation of Hilfield during the First World War. (Jean McIlwaine)

In Eversley, Alice had met her future husband, Leonard Fendall Thompson, a gunner in the Australian Artillery. How did a lady from Yateley meet a gunner from Tasmania? Leonard had been wounded and in and out of hospitals in Egypt and England, but he came to Eversley because his mother had been living at Up Green even before he had embarked from Melbourne with the Australian Expeditionary Force. Emma Fendall Thompson was living with her daughter-in-law, Mrs Ada Verini. Ada Fendall Thompson had married the Rev Philip George Augustine Verini in Lewes in 1889, but she had been a widow since 1898. Mrs Ada Verini was Leonard's sister. She worked at Firgrove Hospital, 'arranging patients needlework, amusements etc whole time Oct 1914 to Jan 1919'. Leonard was shipped back to Australia in May 1917 to be demobbed. Miss Alice Stilwell, then aged 50, took the ship to Australia and married Leonard on 23 December 1918 at St Mark's, Darling Point, Sydney.

Hilfield Lodge was the home of Richard and Annie Sealy. Richard Sealy was the Stilwell's coachman. Just five days before 15 July 1918, their eldest son, Clifford, had been transferred to HMS *Mischief* as a Leading Telegraphist. Their second son, Victor, was 18 on 2 August, joining the Hampshire Regiment for the remainder of the war. He had been Patrol Leader of the Wolves in the 8th Odiham (Yateley) Scouts.

Set back from the main road across a small green were two very old farm cottages. Sydney Loader said that Frank Rapley, who

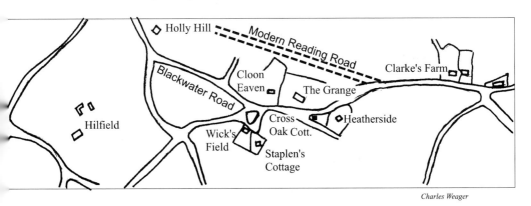

Charles Weager

The main road from Holly Hill to Clarkes Farm was not bypassed until after the Second World War.

lived in the first, was the last man in Yateley to cut peat from the common to burn on his fire. The other house was Staplen's Cottage, now Grade II listed. Edith Miriam Phillips lived there as a widow in 1918. She had moved from Hazeley Heath, where she had raised her family. Her son, Frederick George Phillips, had been working as a butcher in Yateley before the war. He was now registered at Staplen's Cottage as an 'absent voter' serving in the Army Service Corps.

Closer to the road on the same side, Cross Oak Cottage, also thatched, was divided between two families. It is now Grade II listed. In 1918, William and Minnia Freeman lived in one side and Job and Rosina Harris in the other. Job was an old soldier who had been invalided out of the Oxford Light Infantry in 1897. As a National Reservist, he had re-enlisted on 3 September 1914 at the age of 40, joining the 1st Supernumary Company of the 5th Battalion, Hampshire Regiment for Home Service. He was transferred to the Royal Defence Corps when it was formed in April 1916. In July 1918, he was serving with 259 Protection Company. Before the war, he had worked as a labourer for Hampshire County Council.

Job's address in his service papers is given as Heatherside Cottages, because Cross Oak Cottage was then considered to be a tied cottage to the large modern house next-door called Heatherside, now demolished and replaced by post-war houses. This modern four-bedroom house was probably empty in July 1918, as nobody was registered to vote there at that time, or in January 1919. Captain John Philip Clingo moved in in 1920 from the Anchor Inn at Cove. He had married his wife, Maud Gosden, in Cairo in 1910. She was the daughter of the landlord at the Anchor in Hawley. The *London Gazette* of 24 September 1918 carried the citation of the award of his Military Cross:

> '*Lt. (A./Capt.) John Philip Clingo, Linc. R. For conspicuous gallantry and devotion to duty while in charge of a company during an enemy attack. Showing great coolness and ability, he held the position for thirty six hours, and when forced to withdraw took up a position on high ground, collecting a number of stragglers on the way. He set a fine example of courage and good leadership.*'

Cross Oak Cottage is both the ancient and modern name of this thatched cottage on the road we now call Potley Hill. During the Great War it was known as Heatherside Cottages, and was divided into two tenures. The large house on the left, called Heatherside, had been recently built before the First World War. Heatherside has since been demolished and Cross Oak Cottage is Grade II listed. (Jean McIlwaine)

Holly Hill was the home of John Mills, a retired Indian Army surgeon. When he died in 1913, his son, John Coleridge Mills, was studying engineering at London University and his daughter had already joined VAD 94. The family sold the house to Mr A.H. Templer, Chairman of Yateley Parish Council, for £2,100 on 6 January 1914. John Coleridge Mills was killed in action on 25 September 1915, serving with the 19th Highland Light Infantry. Until the 1980s, the house stood at the western end of the road now known as Potley Hill, but was demolished for development as a housing estate. (Jean McIlwaine)

In 1918, there were only three large houses on the north side of the main road: Holly Hill, Cloon Eavin and the Grange. Holly Hill, across the road from Hilfield Lodge, was the home of Arthur Henry Templer, a retired tea planter related to the Mason ladies living in the Croft. Mr Templer was then 58 years old and was Chairman of Yateley Parish Council. Holly Hill was his third residence in Yateley. He had first rented Heathcroft from John Masterman, then Simla until the Vicar moved there when he volunteered the vicarage to be the Military Hospital. Just before the war, Templar had built Cherry Tree Cottages, establishing the Telephone Exchange in one and the Police Constable in the other. The Templars had bought

Cloon Eavin.

Cloon Eavin still stands on the north side of the road now called Potley Hill. It was on the main road in the First World War, owned by J.P. Stilwell, but leased by retired Brigadier-General Wiliam Johnston Kirkpatrick. Following its formation, Kirkpatrick was the first commander of the 43rd (Wessex) Division from April to December 1908. The 1st/4th Hampshire Regiment was one of this division's constituents, being part of the 128th Infantry Brigade. In 1923, Lieutenant Colonel Charles Sumner Stooks DSO took up residence at Cloon Eavin, moving from Camberley. The son of a former vicar of Yateley, he had served in the Indian Army in Africa during the Great War. (Jean McIlwaine)

Holly Hill after John Mills had died in 1913. These moves are a prime example of the way Yateley houses were used as short-term lets during this tumultuous period.

Retired Brigadier General William Johnston Kirkpatrick lived at Cloon Eavin with his family. They were no relation to Surgeon Lieutenant Colonel Henry Kirkpatrick and his family, who later came to live on Cricket Hill before the Second World War. General Kirkpatrick was a Trustee of the Yateley Military Hospital. His son, Major Colin Drummond Kirkpatrick, was award the Military Cross in 1917 serving with the Royal Garrison Artillery. His daughter had married William Shakspeare in 1912.

The next house on the north side of the road was Yateley Grange, the home of Miss Caroline Thoyts. She was the younger sister of Mrs Emma Elizabeth Cope, wife of John Hautenville Cope, the youngest son of Sir William Cope of Bramshill. The Hautenville Copes had lived in Yateley at Little Croft on Handford Lane when he was an editor on the staff of the original *Victoria County History*. Both he and his wife, Emma, were very active researchers for both the Hampshire and Berkshire County Archaeological Societies. Mrs Cope gave lectures in Yateley during the First World War, and Hautenville had been very active in the recruitment in 1914. In contrast, Caroline at the Grange does not appear to have taken any part in community life.

Yateley Grange had been built in 1878 on the site of the ancient Malthouse. The main crops in Yateley had been barley and hops. For two or three centuries from Tudor times, the Malthouse had been owned by the Clark family, who had lived in the ancient farmhouse on Darby Green. Before Miss Thoyts moved there, Yateley Grange had been a crammer run by a Mr Kirchhofer for young men trying to get into Sandhurst. Hautenville Cope had been one of his pupils.

DARBY GREEN

As you walked on from Yateley Grange to Clark's Farm, you would have seen orchards on both sides of the road. It is at this point that you would have perceived the character of the civil parish was changing. In the west of the parish, from Yateley Green to the Grange, the main road had been lined with villas and mansions, interspersed with shops and the homes of artisans, mainly from long-established Yateley families. Eastwards from the Grange, on the northern edge of Darby Green, stood six ancient farms and smallholdings. Clark's Farm, Pond Farm, Pond Cottage and the Willows are now all Grade II listed. Darby Green Farm, for centuries part of the ancient Manor of Hall Place, was demolished to make way for Olde Farm Drive, adopted in July 1969. Yew Tree Cottage, dating from the fifteenth century and probably the oldest of the group, remains unlisted.

Clark's Farm is at the north-eastern tip of Darby Green. From the old road you would see its large bank of five rows of greenhouses behind Yew Tree Cottages. Today, the modern main road slices through the old farmland to the north of Holly Hill, Cloon Eavin and the Grange, rejoining the old main road between the latter and Clark's Farm. In 1918, the farm was in the ownership of the third generation of the Prier family. Henry Robert Prier, who lived there with his wife, Constance, described himself in *Kellys Directory* as 'fruit grower, Darby Green'.

A few yards after the entrance to the farm you will come to a very old half-timbered building split into two cottages in 1918. The Yew Tree Inn had been licensed under the 1872 Beerhouses Act, but the licensing records for the session of the Licensing Magistrates held on 23 August 1881 contains a note saying 'house converted as church'. It was John Mills of Holly Hill who had been instrumental in turning the pub's tap-room into the Darby Green Mission of St Peter's Yateley for the benefit of parishoners at the eastern end of the parish. In 1905, he obtained a corrugated iron mission church of the sort exported all over the Empire. The 'tin church' stood on its rectangle of common land until the 1990s.

Robert James Ruffle was a private who served with the 4th Hants. As a Territorial, he was called-up for war service on 5 August 1914, and given the option of serving abroad. His army service papers record Yew Tree Cottage, Darby Green, as the address of his next of kin, his father, James. When he had first signed up as a Territorial on 20 January 1914, he stated his last employer had been Mr Ireland at Pond Farm. The attesting officer had been John Grant Stilwell and the recruiting officer William Byron Stilwell, Jack Stilwell's uncle. Robert Ruffle gave his age as 17 years and

3 months. This young man was probably just 18 when he sailed for India on 9 October 1914.

When he enlisted into F Company, 4th Hants in January 1914, Robert Ruffle could not have foreseen that almost exactly three years later he would be shot in the right arm, fracturing his humerus, in Mesopotamia, a country he probably only knew about from Bible stories, nor thought that he would have to spend over a year in hospitals in India and Bristol.

The village Pound was across Darby Green from the mission church. The Pound was used to collect stray animals found on Yateley Common until their owners claimed them. In the distance, beyond the Pound on the rising ground, was Old Cottage, the childhood home of Sydney Loader, then 13 years old. We have to thank Sydney for writing his memoirs and preserving letters and documents from this period. In 1976, he had a brief correspondence with John Parker Whitehorn, who was born on 16 March 1900. During the First World War, Whitehorn lived nearby at Sunnyside, which you will pass shortly. About the area around Clark's Farm he wrote:

> '*The Priers family, was living at Clarks farm, when I was a boy. As the road outside, was so very muddy, we had to walk on our heels, when going to chapel on Sunday ... Pond Farm was, before the first world war, two cottages, a Mr Elijah James lived in one of them.*'

By 1918, Pond Farm was still split into two cottages, Elijah James had gone and two newcomers, Henry Polden and John Butler, were living there with their wives. Henry Polden was an 'absent voter'. Today, Pond Farm is a listed building in single occupancy.

Anthony Ireland, mentioned in Robert Ruffle's attestation as the occupant of the other half of the farmhouse in 1914, had moved to Ivydene in Frogmore. His 18-year-old son, Arthur Percy Thomas Ireland, had enlisted in 1917 in the Yorkshire Regiment as a motor driver. He had learnt to drive working for Joby James' haulage business in Blackwater. In April 1918, Arthur Ireland had transferred to the RAF to become a Sergeant Pilot.

A postwar photograph of Pond Farm to the north of Darby Green. Now a listed building in single ownership, the house was divided into two tenures during the First World War and occupied by farm workers. (Jean McIlwaine)

Written on the back of this postcard in Sydney Loader's handwriting is 'I am one of the boys paddling'. Cornelius Charles Bartlett lived in the thatched Pond Cottage, on the left, with his wife, (Matilda) Elizabeth. Born in 1853, Bartlett described himself as a smallholder in the 1911 census. Pond Cottage is now a Grade II listed building. (Jean McIlwaine)

Darby Green Yateley   C160

The road towards the Greyhound public house has a pond on your right and an old thatched cottage on your left. Cornelius Charles Bartlett, a 65-year-old smallholder, lived there with his wife, Matilda Elizabeth. John Parker Whitehorn wrote in 1976:

'At the top of the pond facing Pond Cottage, there used to be a well of drinking water where old Mr Bartlett used to get his drinking water, and I have often seen him walking with pails of it.

'Once Mother ran out of the house with one of us (a baby) in her arms during a big common fire and the sparks were blowing over our roof. I remember seeing old Mr Cornelius Bartlett and his wife struggling across the road with pails of water from the pond and throwing it over their thatched roof at Pond Cottage. They also had to fetch all their water from a well about 50 yards across the common near the head of the pond. The Bartletts had lived in the cottage for many years, possibly 200. After they died the cottage was altered and enlarged, and once the new owners saw an apparition of Mrs Bartlett coming down the stairs and looking very annoyed.'

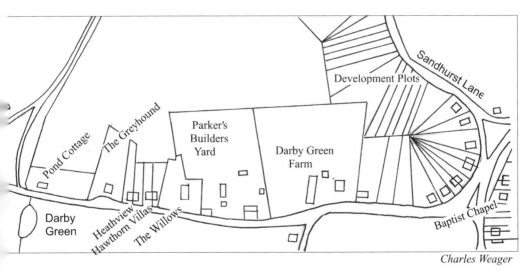

Charles Weager

The road from Darby Green pond to the junction of Rosemary Lane and Frogmore Road ran along the north side of Darby Green.

According to Sydney Ireson Loader in 1981:

> '*We had to cross the common, not easy in the winter when there was [sic] pools of water, much mud and many boggy places. When it was frozen over there were plenty of places to slide, besides Bartlett's Pond. Now that part of the common has been made into a football ground.*'

The Land Tax assessors noted in 1910 that the Greyhound had two bars, was newly built by Mr Richard Kelsey about four years ago and was in good repair. The previous building had been burnt down. In 1912, Kelsey, one of the largest landowners in Yateley, complained in a letter to his solicitors: 'A new house and a new tenant should help the house a good deal, but the present tenant is not what he should be the Beer is not so good as it ought to be either, that is not improving things much.' It seems that Headingtons, the Wokingham brewers, did change their tenant, who was Dorcas Spencer, in 1918.

The Greyhound Inn shown here was built just before the First World War by Richard Kelsey to replace the original pub at the Willows, now Grade II listed. Kelsey lived in Eversley, but he was Yateley's largest landowner. As well as owning large farms managed by tenants, he also developed new housing estates, such as that at Lowlands Road. (Philip Todd)

Darby Green.

The old Baptist Church on Cricket Hill during the First World War before it was rebuilt. The sale by George Searle of a 'plot of land whereon a Chapel is erected' was recorded in the Manorial Court Books of Crondall Manor on 1 March 1827. (Jean McIlwaine)

Facing the open common land to the south was a number of houses owned by the Parker family. The late Ken Walters, a leading member of the Baptist Church on Cricket Hill and a member of the research team for this book, wrote:

'During this period the Parker family played a major part in the life of the Baptist Church on Cricket Hill, and the local community. At least fifteen of the family were members or attendees of the church.

'George Parker senior (b. 1850) was the founder of George Parker and Sons who were carpenters, blacksmiths, wheelwrights, builders and undertakers. George had four sons and a daughter, Herbert, Charles, George Harry, Sidney and Lily, all of whom with their respective spouses were members of the church. Most of these were present at the wedding at the turn of the century of Lily Jane Parker (b. 2 July 1878) to Jack Whitehorn.

'George Parker senior was a carpenter and wheelwright. Herbert was a carpenter. Charles William was a carpenter, house painter and decorator, and was also involved in the *funeral business. George Harry was the blacksmith and undertaker. Sidney James was a wheelwright and in the funeral business. Lily's husband was also a carpenter and coffin maker.'*

The first houses beyond the Greyhound are both semi-detached. The first pair was built by George Parker senior in 1899. He built the other pair, Hawthorn Villas, in 1910 for two of his sons.

The young John Parker Whitehorn, whose 'Dear Syd' letters we are quoting, was living in the half of the older pair known as Sunnyside with his parents, John and Lily Whitehorn née Parker: 'The day they put the chimney pots on, and hoisted the red flag, was May 24th 1899, my mum's wedding day.'

Herbert Parker had lived next-door at Heatherview, but in 1918 Albert Edward Capell was living there with his wife, Florence. When he volunteered to join the Royal Flying Corps under the Derby Scheme in 1915, he was working as a joiner, probably for the Parkers. When the Royal Air Force was founded on 1 April 1918 by amalgamating the Royal Flying Corps with the Royal Naval Air Service, Albert Capell and the other Yateley men working at Farnborough were transferred to the RAF.

Next-door to Hawthorn Villas was The Willows. This half timbered and thatched old house had been the original Greyhound beerhouse. After a series of bankruptcies, it had been purchased in 1882 by John, the father of George Parker senior, who had been a tenant for a few year previously but now, in 1918, had moved to a newly built house next-door to the east called Southlands. His son, George Harry Parker, was living at the Willows with his family.

Next-door to Southlands was the ancient farmhouse of Darby Green Farm, which had been part of the Manor of Hall Place for centuries. No longer a farmhouse, the property had been bought in August 1900 by Mrs Alice Singer. She and her husband, Julius, a London wine and spirits merchant, had lived there until September 1907, when they signed a lease for seven years with Dr John MacCormac. During the suffragette campaign of political protest in 1912, Alice Singer, who was by then an ardent suffragette, had been arrested for smashing three windows in the West Strand Telegraph

This gravestone of Roy the dog, who died in May 1913, is on Yateley Common near the Haywarden's House in Frogmore. VM, the initials of his mistress, was the clue which enabled us to discover that her husband, Surgeon-Lieutenant John Sides Davies MacCormac, was killed at the Battle of Jutland aboard HMS Black Prince. *His wife, Genevieve (Viva), moved to Cornwall shortly after his death. (Tony Beveridge)*

Office close to Trafalgar Square. She was brought to court from Holloway Prison on 13 March. As she had a small child, and unlike most of the other women who were given jail sentences, Alice was released bound over to keep the peace.

In November 1914, Dr John Sides Davies MacCormac had volunteered for service in the Royal Navy. He was the anaesthetist aboard HMS *Black Prince* when this armoured cruiser was sunk with all hands during the Battle of Jutland in 1916.

By 1918 the conscription of young men reaching their 18th birthday resulted in some fathers and their sons serving in the war. One family, the O'Rourkes of Rosemary Lane, had father and three sons serving.

William and Bridget O'Rourke had arrived in Yateley before the 1911 census. Before the war, O'Rourke was a live-in cook for the MacCormacs at Darby Green Farm. His family were living in a very small cottage on Rosemary Lane owned by E.J. Capner of

York Town. It only had four rooms and a wash house, and was in poor repair.

William Andrew O'Rourke, the father, was 42 years old when he re-enlisted on 22 August 1914. He declared he was only 40 and had previously served for twelve years in the 2nd Battalion, The Black Watch. He was posted to the 6th (Service Company) Queen's Royal West Surrey Regiment and was immediately promoted to sergeant. A year later, he was promoted to company sergeant major in the 10th Battalion, the Queen's, and served in France. When the Labour Corps was created in 1917, he was transferred as CSM to the 301st Works Company back in England. When demobbed in 1919, he had spent almost thirty years, on and off, in the Army, fought in the Boer War in South Africa, the Great War in France and had earned his Silver War Badge.

Two of Sergeant Major O'Rourke's sons served in the Great War and a third son, the youngest, was an 'absent voter' in 1921.

After Mrs Viva MacCormac had lost her husband at Jutland, she left Yateley. The Singers then arranged to lease Darby Green Farm on a series of short-term lets. On 15 July 1918, the occupant was Harold Beresford Butler, then playing a significant role as a senior civil servant in the Ministry of Labour established by the New Ministries and Secretaries Act 1916. His brother had taken a short-term lease of The Croft from the Misses Mason. By January 1919, Lieutenant Charles Gough Howell of the Royal Field Artillery had replaced Butler at Darby Green Farm, and the Mason ladies had moved back into The Croft. Major Rene Bull quickly became the Singers' third tenant. All three have very interesting life stories. These four men illustrate the wide availability of short-term lets in Yateley, which were taken up by all manner and sorts of people.

FROGMORE

East of Darby Green Farm, the character of the parish changes yet again. This third area is characterized by the new housing built since the turn of the century. The residents were therefore largely newcomers to the parish.

You will reach a T-junction after a short walk. The left fork is Rosemary Lane; Sandhurst Lane is an immediate left fork off Rosemary Lane. In 1918, there was a crescent of recently built housing spreading from Darby Green Farm, into Rosemary Lane and along the southern side of Sandhurst Lane. The earliest of these houses in Darby Green Road already had their own individual names: Violet Cottage, Albert Cottage, Rose Cottage. No.1 The Crescent was the name of the first new semi-detached house, which was then owned by John Brinn and occupied by Charles Broomfield. The other half of this semi (No.2) was named Hope Cottage. None of the other new houses (twenty-seven in total) was named in the Electoral Registers: the occupants were simply recorded as living at The Crescent, Frogmore. One third of the adult occupants of The Crescent served in uniform in the First World War.

Directly in front of you across the T-junction was a Baptist Chapel, which had no connection with the Zoar Baptist Church

Frogmore Baptist Church was at the junction of Frogmore Road and Rosemary Lane. This photograph of the congregation, taken in 1927, shows the church, which was associated with the Camberley Baptist Church and not that on Cricket Hill. (Jean McIlwaine)

on Cricket Hill, nor the Parker family. Behind the Baptist Chapel to the east was Rosemary Farm, skirted to the north by Rosemary Lane and to the south by Frogmore Road. Two brothers, William and John Chitty, had inherited the farm and split the land between them. John Chitty's house, called New Farm, was just around the corner from the T-junction, on the southern side of Rosemary Lane, but there was access to the fields from Frogmore Road.

John Parker Whitehorn recalled on 21 January 1976:

'The best gravel pit of the district was behind Mr John Chitty's house. In the first world war a firm from Reading named Talbot, worked it, and they took tons of gravel to the Royal Aircraft Factory at Farnborough.

'They used traction engines, towing trucks of sand, and it made the road from the pit to the top of Frogmore Road so muddy that Talbots had to keep putting gravel down to get their traction engines on the move.'

William Tice noted that there was 'much needed rain' on 10 July after '3 weeks beautiful weather after June 24'. As the runways at Farnborough had already been completed well before 1918, the surface of Frogmore Road should be back to its pre-war state during your walk on Monday 15 July, as you take the right fork in Frogmore Road to pass the entrance to the gravel pit, eventually reaching the Bell public house.

Before reaching the Bell Inn, you would already have formed the impression of Frogmore as a thriving commercial community, independent of Yateley, although still remaining in the same Civil Parish. Not far along Frogmore Road, you would pass on your left the workshops of Thomas Turner, another local builder and contractor. There were at least five building firms operating in Darby Green and Frogmore. Even Brake Brothers, the large developer of Fleet, was sharing in the pre-war building boom in Sandhurst Lane. Frogmore had several landlords who had invested in many of the new properties to provide themselves with rental income. Brinns Lane is named after John Brinn, who owned most of the houses along it. Living at one of the several Yateley houses named Sunnyside at the eastern end, Brinn was a gardener retired from working at Hart's Leap in Sandhurst. He was born at Kidmore End in Oxfordshire. It is not clear where his capital had come from, but his son, Joseph, had also invested in houses in Frogmore.

John Elliott the greengrocer grew his produce in three greenhouses on the south side of the road, facing a small green on the other side. Across the green to the left of the entrance to Brinns Lane was Frogmore Cottage. Frederick Charles Mustow was living there in 1918 with his wife, Margaret. He was the brother-in-law of the ill-fated Cecilia Mustow née Agar.

On the right, as Frogmore Road enters Frogmore Green, was Frogmore Post Office, run by Alfred Beeson and his wife, Charlotte. Before they came to Frogmore, they had run a grocery shop in Windsor, so their main business was selling groceries. Their son, also named Alfred, was away serving in the Army in the Coldstream Guards. He had been a Police Constable in Cove before the war.

A postwar photograph of Frogmore Post Office and general stores. John Whitehorn, whose letters to Sydney Loader are quoted in this book, is the person with the delivery bike. Alfred Beeson, the postmaster during the First World War, had been replaced by Willam Barranger Trowbridge by 1924. (Gordon Harland)

Miss Lucy Mary Beeson in Post Office uniform. Lucy was the daughter of Alfred Beeson, the postmaster, and his wife, Charlotte Mary. The 1911 census describes Lucy as 'assistant in business'. Her brother, Alfred, was Police Constable 443 based in Cove before the war, joining up as Guardsman 27895 in the Coldstreams. (Jean McIlwaine)

The Beesons had direct competition right across the road. Mrs Kate Boyce was first listed in *Kelly's Directory* as a grocer in Frogmore in 1915. Her husband was a Dubliner and a major retired from the Warwickshire Regiment. They had lived at Langdale, next door to the Bell, since before the war. Perhaps they spotted a business opportunity resulting from the pre-war housing boom.

In the 1891 census there were only thirty-one heads of households in the whole of Frogmore. By 1910, the Land Tax Assessors were able to tax nineteen houses in just the small triangular block bounded by Frogmore Road, Brinns Lane and Bell Lane. There was a similar block of twenty-one new houses which had been built just across Frogmore Green from the Boyces' grocery shop. The nearest, Gordon Villas, had been built in 1908. Even closer to the Boyces, in the same block as Alfred Beeson's shop, was a block of twelve new houses, six of them owned by John Brinn. In the 1911 census, seventy-two householders gave Frogmore as their address

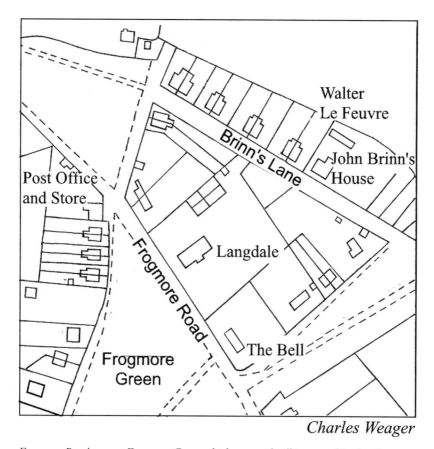

Charles Weager

Frogmore Road crosses Frogmore Green which was, and still is, part of Yateley Common.

and another fifteen lived in Rosemary Lane. The village had trebled in size in under thirty years.

In 1911, only 12 per cent of heads of households in Frogmore had been born in Yateley, whereas across the whole civil parish the total was 20 per cent. The pre-war adult population of Frogmore was therefore mostly incomers. This state is not likely to have changed during the war, as servicemen moved into the area during this time. For instance, Percy Frank Heath Ferguson, a director of the London wine merchants Walter Symons, was living in Brighton in 1911. In 1918, he lived at Ingleside in Frogmore whilst serving as a captain in the Army Service Corps.

Alice Maude Bodger was another recent arrival. In July 1918, she was living with her three children at 2 The Flats Cottages, Frogmore. The most recent addition to the family was Irene Lucy, born in Farnham on 5 January 1916. Robert John Bodger was an 'Old Contemptible', having gone to France with the Army Service Corps on 15 August 1914. He had had nine months back in England in 1915, but was now in France again. When he was discharged to Frogmore in March 1919, he had earned an excellent testimonial: 'a good driver, groom and NCO. He is willing and hardworking, honest, sober and reliable, and gave satisfaction.' However, he had an interesting personal history. Eight months after he was attested into the Army Service Corps in 1900, he made a confession:

> *'I no.16260 Driver Bodger R.J. do hereby confess that I am John Bodger, AB 1st Class Seaman Gunner, Royal Navy, and that I deserted from HMS* Pelican *about July 1896 at Port Royal, Jamaica, West Indies.'*

The Bell Inn at Frogmore was run by Mr Lewis Damrel. Born in Buckland Filleigh, near Torrington in North Devon, he was 70 years old in 1918. He and his wife, Grace, had been running the Bell since before 1891. Before becoming a publican he had been the butler at Oakley Hall in Deane near Basingstoke. (Jean McIlwaine)

Bell Inn Frogmore

The Bell Inn, next-door to Mrs Boyce's shop, had been established as a beer house in about 1862 under the first Beerhouse Act 1830. After 1872, the Bell obtained a full licence to sell beer and cider. Damrel Lewis was 'mine host' in 1918.

After crossing the end of Bell Lane, still then really just a footpath, there was a property on the left owned by Charles Cranham. He lived at The Poplars, and John Parker Whitehorn recalled in 1972:

On my way to Hawley school, I passed the yard of Cranhams builders, it was founded in 1868, 28 years after John Parkers shop ... Before the first world war the Frogmore Road was very low and when the pond on the opposite side of the Poplar Bungalow, flooded the road we, on our way to Hawley school, had to walk on our heels to get through.'

The last house on that side of Frogmore Road was Kent Cottage, the home of James and Charlotte Coombes. James was another bricklayer. One of their sons, Alfred John Coombes, reached his 18th birthday on 9 March 1918, and had just been called up for basic training in the 3rd (Reserve) Battalion of the Hampshire Regiment. The eldest son, William James Charles Coombes, was already serving.

Across Frogmore Green stood Hillside Cottages, two pairs of semi-detached houses built in the back garden of Hillside, a larger house facing Reading Road. They were all owned by Thomas Douse senior, who lived at Hillside with his wife, Catherine. They were also incomers. Thomas was a retired coachman from Corsham in Wiltshire. Their son, Thomas Arthur Douse, born in Swallowfield, was 28 years old when he volunteered for the Royal Engineers in March 1915. At the time he was employed as a ship's joiner by Glengall Iron Works Limited, who operated two drydocks at Millwall on London's Isle of Dogs.

Thomas Douse junior served three periods in France, being hospitalized back to England each time. In April 1918, after the third time he was injured, he was shipped back to England to the Military Hospital in York with a shell wound to his right thigh.

Much later he received a Silver War Badge. By 4 June, he was considered fit enough for civilian war service. He elected to work at Smith Dock Company in Middlesborough until the end of the war.

Reaching the main Reading to Aldershot road, you would have seen a semi-detached house in front of you at the entrance to Lowlands Road. Built in 1905, Sunlea was owned by Joseph Brinn, the son of John Brinn of Brinns Lane. Other pre-war houses had been built on Lowlands Road, but contemporary records mostly simply gave their address as The Flats, Blackwater. Including the four dwellings which had been the farmhouse and cottages of Bailey's Farm, sixteen families had lived on The Flats in 1911. The 1918 Electoral Register included twenty-two families on the same development, including the names of sixteen servicemen registered as 'absent voters'.

Charles Callas Wooldridge, killed during the Battle of the Somme on 1 October 1916, had lived with his wife in one of the old cottages of Bailey's Farm. Three more servicemen were born in Yateley, but all the rest were newcomers, including one born in Australia.

Just before the war, new housing was built on the edge of the common in Frogmore on land known as Bailey's Farm, owned by Richard Kelsey of Eversley. Plots were sold at £200 per acre. John Bailey, who died in 1862, was a London poulterer and the step-grandfather of Sir Thomas Sturmy Cave, colonel of the 4th Battalion, Hampshire Regiment, before 1914. (Gordon Harland)

The Flats, Blackwater.

Frogmore Park had two lodges. The South Lodge, seen here, provided access onto Frogmore Road. In 1918, William and May Bailey lived in one lodge, with Herbert and Ellen Gale in the other. (Gordon Harland)

The southern lodge of Frogmore Park, the Fitzroys' large house, was on the north side of the main Reading road towards Blackwater. Another newcomer, at the other end of the social scale, had recently moved into Frogmore Park with his wife. Lieutenant Colonel Alfred Nathaniel Curzon was the brother of Lord Curzon, former Viceroy of India and now member of Lloyd George's War Cabinet. Lieutenant Colonel Curzon commanded the 3rd Battalion, the Sherwood Foresters, a reserve battalion which formed part of the East Coast Defences. Frogmore Park was available for short-term lease following the death at 88 of the Hon. Gertrude Fitzroy on 24 February 1916. Her eldest son, Sir Almeric, remained as Clerk to the Privy Council (equivalent to Permanent Secretary), necessitating his continued residence at the Fitzroys' London address in Belgravia.

Walking towards the main road (now the A30), you would have seen another large house called Hurstleigh on your left. The boundary between the civil parishes of Yateley and Hawley was said to run through its living room. Hurstleigh was the home of. Rear-Admiral Herbert William Sumner Gibson who was promoted

Hurstleigh was the home of retired Admiral Herbert Gibson in the Great War. This very old site of habitation had been the home of the admiral's mother, Louisanna, the elder daughter of Charles Sumner, Bishop of Winchester, and niece of John Sumner, Archbishop of Canterbury. Admiral Gibson was therefore a close relative of Rev C.D. Stooks, Vicar of Yateley until 1905, whose family returned to live in Yateley after the First World War. (Gordon Harland)

to vice-admiral on 6 December 1905 in the same notice which promoted Admiral Jackie Fisher to Admiral of the Fleet. Admiral Gibson had inherited Hurstleigh from his mother, a daughter of Charles Sumner, a former Bishop of Winchester. Admiral Gibson was therefore a first cousin of the wife of the Rev Charles Drummond Stooks, who retired as Vicar of Yateley in the same year that Gibson was promoted to vice-admiral.

HOLLY TREE COTTAGES

Looking at Hurstleigh from the junction of the Reading to Aldershot road with the main London to Exeter road, you would notice a couple of smaller houses in your sight-line, nearer to you. These were Holly Tree Cottages, owned by the Hurstleigh Estate.

Your walk ends here, at the parish boundary with Hawley. However there is quite a story to tell about two families who lived in one of these two semi-detached cottages, the nearest to the main London Road.

ckwater Cross Roads.

The Reading to Aldershot road crossed the main road from London to the West Country at Blackwater cross roads. There is a large roundabout there today. Hurstleigh, the home of Admiral Gibson during the First World War, stands behind the trees to the left of the service station. During the Great War, Hurstleigh was still in Yateley Civil Parish, although today its site is in Blackwater and Hawley Civil Parish. (Jean McIlwaine)

The 1891 census records Edward Mustow living at Holly Tree Cottages with his growing family. He had been born in Cirencester, and his wife, Sarah, was born in Mapledurham. They had married in 1868 but had arrived in Hawley by 1871, where he took his first post as butler. In 1881, he and his family were living in the Butler's House at Hawley Hill, just across the main London road. By 1901, Admiral Gibson (then still a captain) had taken up residence at Hurstleigh and the Hoare family had replaced the Mustows in Holly Tree Cottages. Walter Hoare was a carpenter and joiner.

In 1911, about 10 per cent of houses in the Civil Parish employed at least one live-in domestic servant. However, even during the previous fifty years, not many of Yateley's grand houses had employed butlers; only two did so in 1911. J.P. Stilwell's father-in-law employed a butler in 1861 at Hilfield, as did Lieutenant Colonel John Grimes, who was then renting Yateley Hall. A butler was employed by Samuel Kirchhoffer at Yateley Grange when he ran it as a crammer for entry at Sandhurst. There was always a butler at Yateley Lodge and Frogmore House, but never, it seems, at Yateley Manor, where an all-female staff was preferred. Miss de Winton Corry also preferred all-female indoor staff at Yateley Hall to serve the all-female household.

Mrs Louisanna Gibson, Admiral Gibson's mother, employed a butler as one of her six domestic staff when she purchased Hurstleigh in 1881. Lewis Blunden was the live-in butler recorded on both the 1881 and 1891 Yateley census. Horatio Fitzroy's butler at Frogmore House in 1891 was Frederick Crick. If both houses had named butlers, it is difficult to see where Edward Mustow worked when he lived at Holly Tree Cottage with his family in 1891; perhaps across the main road at Hawley Hill. However, in 1911 he is listed at the top of the eight live-in staff at Frogmore House, although his role was not specified. By that time his wife was dead and his son, Arthur George Mustow, had just married Cecilia Agar, as her first husband.

Together with Henry Hilton, who died in 1918, the deaths of Lady Fitzroy in 1916 and Edward Mustow, her last butler (d. 1917), heralded the end of the old order in Yateley. Henry Hilton had retired as the last hereditary Parish Clerk in 1894, when the church ceased controlling the civil administration of the parish. Mrs Gertrude Fitzroy was one of the last remaining owners of large houses and large estates, who also maintained another London house at a fashionable address. Edward Mustow represents the dying breed of domestic servants. This is not to say that these changes were caused by the Great War, but the landed gentry never recovered in Yateley as a result of the war.

The story of Holly Tree Cottage can be continued with the Hoare family. With the spotlight in 1918 on the Western Front, it should not be forgotten that the 1st/4th Hampshires, including Yateley men, were still fighting Turkish forces in the Middle East. One of those men was Private Arthur Jesse Hoare from Holly Tree Cottage. His parents were Walter and Annie Hoare, who had moved in after Edward Mustow left. The Hoares had arrived from London in the

1890s. Walter was a joiner working for a local builder and Annie was a registered midwife. Annie had borne ten children herself, of whom eight had survived: four boys and four girls. All four boys served in the First World War.

Walter, the eldest, was a stoker in the Royal Navy aboard HMS *Minotaur* at the Battle of Jutland. This light cruiser was positioned so that it could never fire its guns at the German fleet. In 1918, Walter was an acting leading stoker, still on *Minotaur*, now assigned to the Northern Patrol. Walter had joined the Navy in 1915, but Thomas, the second son, had waited until 1917 to join the Royal Flying Corps as an air mechanic. In July 1918, he was with 250 Squadron who were flying anti-submarine patrols over the Bristol Channel.

In July 1918, Annie Hoare would have been grieving the recent loss of her third son. Harold Ernest Hoare, always known as Ernest, had been killed in France on 10 March 1918 serving with the 2nd/5th The Loyal North Lancashire Regiment. He had signed up as a territorial with the Cheshire Regiment on 25 September 1914. Why he was in Chester when he enlisted is not known. When his mother received his effects in May 1918, including a photograph and letters, she added in her own handwriting on the official card acknowledging their receipt, 'PS I am most grateful to you for sending my poor boy's belongings.'

Annie lost her youngest son, Arthur Jesse Hoare, in Persia on 17 October 1918. He is remembered on the Tehran Memorial locked away in the British Embassy. The existing records do not say where or why he died. He was baptized at Holy Trinity Hawley on 6 June 1897, so he could have been only 17 years of age when he sailed for India in 1914 with the other Yateley boys of the 4th Hants. To have survived until thirteen days before Turkey signed its peace agreement with the Allies at Mudros means that Arthur had endured in their entirety all the battles, traumas and diseases which befell his battalion.

Annie Hoare would have been told how Arthur died, but we can only speculate that he died from influenza, which was then rampant in the ports along the Persian Gulf. Annie lived in the last house in the parish and was the last mother living in the Civil Parish to lose a son, having already lost another son seven months earlier.

RÈVE DE BONHEUR.

O dream of lips incarnadine and perfumed breath,
Why do you haunt me in the land of death ?
O laughter sweet, and eyes of azure fire,
Why do you haunt me struggling in the mire ?

Love's whisper mingles with the pattering rain,
And through the wind I hear love's sigh again.
O dream of other days, you've lost your way ;
For here are only sandbags, death, and—clay.

R.R.M.W.

Ploegsteert Wood.

In Loving Memory

OF

ERNEST HOARE,

Who gave his life for his country in France,

On March 10th, 1918,

Aged 23 Years.

Sleep on, beloved, and take thy rest ;
We love you dearly, but God loves you best.

(courtesy of Malcolm Miller)

The War ends for the 4th Hants in the Middle East

Arthur Hoare's service number in the 4th Hants was 4/2894. It is instructive to look at the records of the men with service numbers each side of Arthur's number, five up and five down. These ten men all enlisted with him into the 1st/4ths at Bustard Camp on Salisbury Plain in early September 1914. Two were from Yateley: Harold Carlton Smith (4/2895) was a Camberley garage proprietor who lived in Darby Green, and Alfred Henry Singer (4/2891) had worked as a butcher, living in Mill Lane. Of the eleven men, four died in combat.

Two of the eleven men were from Aldershot, and both were killed. William Edward Frederick Goodrich (4/2901) was killed in action on 24 July 1915. He had been an apprentice letter-press printer. Sydney Applegate (4/2900) had been mentioned in dispatches for his part in the Euphrates operations of 26-27 July 1915, but was killed on 24 February 1917.

Survival of service records for the Yateley men serving in Mesopotamia is rare. We have already mentioned those of Robert James Ruffle (4/2256) from Yew Tree Cottage, who spent over a year in hospitals in India and Bristol. Service papers also still exist for Corporal Charles Marshall (4/1951). He had worked in Frogmore as a builder's labourer for Thomas Turner, and was mentioned in despatches in the same notice as Sydney Applegate from Aldershot. There are also service records for Edward Harry

William Potter (4/2028), who lived at Albert Cottage in Darby Green. He was transferred to the 1st/5th Buffs in the Middle East. Bertram Bunch (4/2161) enlisted on 15 July 1913 in Yateley. He was sent to Mesopotamia with the 1st/4th Hants, was admitted to the British General Hospital in Basrah with a sprained ankle, transferred to the Devon Regiment, sent to Egypt, caught malaria and ended the war in the Labour Corps in Egypt. None of these four men was included in the same sequence of service numbers as Arthur Hoare.

Of the eleven men in our sample of the 4th Hants, it is the service record of Morris Lunn (4/2898) which confirms the awful conditions in the Middle East for the seven survivors. His father had been 'mine host' at the Crown & Cushion on Minley Road who, during the war, was living in Sandy Lane, Hawley. Morris had been one of the staff at Minley Manor in the Yateley Company who volunteered at the outbreak of war. His records show that he was dispatched home because of 'sickness', was then discharged on 19 December 1916 and awarded the Silver War Badge on 8 January 1917 to prove he was not evading conscription.

Two of the eleven were Eversley men, and it is their records which give us an even better picture of the harsh conditions which Arthur Hoare and his Yateley colleagues must have endured. William George Hobby (4/2890) died of his wounds on 25 February 1917, but Herbert James Webb (4/2897) survived. Luckily, Herbert Webb's full discharge papers survive to this day because he claimed for a war disability. He was not discharged until 6 July 1919 but, unlike Arthur, he did not get posted to Persia because he was shipped from Mesopotamia to India in August 1918.

Herbert Webb was injured in the left hand on 20 June 1916 on the regimental barge in Amara. Major W.B. Stilwell signed the injury report, stating it was an accident, not his own fault. In his disability claim in his own handwriting, Herbert Webb stated he had caught malaria about 20 June 1916. His records state he had been admitted to 23 Stationary Hospital in Amara on 31 May and, on 25 June, had been transferred to India, where he spent four months, probably in Deolali Military Hospital near Bombay. Having returned to the front in Mesopotamia, his records state he had colitis on '16 July 1917 caused by heat and bad water'. A year later this condition had become so severe that he was admitted to hospital in Baghdad, transferred to Basrah Hospital on 15 August, and then on again to India from where he was shipped back for discharge to England ten months later.

By looking at the records of these eleven men collectively, we can see that they all enlisted at Bustard Camp on Salisbury Plain between 3-5 September 1914. The Yateley and Eversley men had not trained before the war with F Company at Yateley Drill Hall, but had rallied to the flag at its outbreak. Rather than join Kitchener's New Armies, they had joined their fellow villagers in the local territorial regiment. The deaths of four out of the eleven men in this small random sample is three times the average national death rate.

They all signed up before Turkey entered the war on 29 October 1914. Had these eleven men known in advance what was to befall them, would they still have willingly signed up to serve abroad? They believed their role was to garrison the Empire to enable Regular troops to fight in France. They certainly knew they would

This photograph of the pony and mule lines at Kolpur Camp in India was sent home to his mother by Sergeant George Reginald Cranham of London Road, Blackwater. He was serving with the 4th Hants in Quetta. Kolpur, now in the Baluchistan Province of Pakistan, is at an altitude of nearly 7,000ft. (Yvonne Allen).

not be 'home for Christmas', because they would not even have reached their destination by Christmas 1914.

Their war was not on the Western Front but in Mesopotamia, now Iraq. They endured harsh fighting, extremes of temperature and sickness from diseases they probably had never heard of before they signed up.

We started our story of the 4th Hants in 1914 with Cyril Bunch and the Butler boys enjoying a bell-ringing expedition from Bustard Camp on Salisbury Plain. Cyril Bunch (4/1576) left Yateley in the ranks of F Company, 4th Hants, but arrived home as an officer in the RAF, having flown his Sopwith Camel in Macedonia for about a month before Turkey surrendered on 30 October 1918. He was unlucky enough to catch the 'flu in mid-November. From Greece he was transferred first to a hospital in Italy, then on to the General Hospital in Rouen and Battle Hospital (then a military hospital) in Reading. His recovery at the Royal Berks Hospital in Reading took months. Cyril Bunch was finally demobilized on 7 June 1919. Those men who survived the fighting and influenza epidemic in the Middle East might have been surprised to arrive home to learn the 'flu had reached the population in Great Britain.

While serving in Egypt, Cyril Bunch transferred from the 4th Hants to be commissioned in the newly formed RAF to train as a pilot. After qualifying to wear his 'wings' on 14 September 1918, he was posted to 150 Squadron at Keric in Macedonia. He notes in his logbook that he flew his Sopwith Camel on a patrol on 29 September 1918 to Lake Dorian. This was the day before Bulgaria surrendered; Turkey surrendered a month later. Cyril Bunch became seriously ill with Spanish flu on 17 November 1918, like so many others serving on the Salonika Front. He was treated in a succession of hospitals for many months before being well enough to be demobbed in June 1919. (Christopher Bunch)

Spanish 'Flu

The burial registers of St Peter's Yateley do not record any increase in deaths of local people in 1918 which might have been attributed to the influenza epidemic. That the epidemic was of grave concern in Yateley is evidenced by the closure of the village school for almost a month until 25 November, as shown by the School Log Book of 29 October 1918:

> *'Still more [children] absent this morning.*
> * 1.15 No school this afternoon on account of wire from Dr Syster ordering closure of school on account of influenza.'*

Sydney Loader gives us a harrowing account from the other end of the civil parish:

> *'I well remember the terrible epidemic of influenza in, I think, 1918. Nearly everyone caught it and it was deadly. Mrs [Susan] Baldwin of Lowlands Road died and several of her children. Of the Passingham family at Starveacre only the father and a little girl of about two were left and the father went and drowned himself in Minley Lake. About a year later old Mrs Scuffle of Hornley Farm also threw herself in the lake in a fit of depression and was drowned. She and her granddaughter Amy had worked in the manor gardens and Amy was in my class at school. Old Mr Scuffle and one of his sons were gardeners on the Plain, the pleasant garden of the Manor.'*

Mrs Susan Baldwin was the wife of William David Baldwin of Trevereux, Flat Cottages, Frogmore, and a sister of Job Harris from Cross Oak Cottage. William Baldwin had been called up on 8 February 1917 to serve in the Royal Field Artillery. However, he was placed on the reserve list on 10 July on condition he work for James & Holford at Wellington College. He was a sawyer and steam saw operator. He was at home at the time of his wife's death and was formally discharged from the Army on 14 December 1918.

There are death certificates for five members of the Passingham family. Frank Passingham was 42 and his wife Catherine 37.

William George Hudson, son of the proprietor of Yateley's first taxi service, died in Greece on 16 January 1919. Graham Fleuty suggests in his book that William may well have died in the great influenza epidemic, which ultimately took more lives than combat in the Great War. There are 500 soldiers buried in the Commonwealth War Graves Commission Mikra Cemetery who died between December 1918 and February 1919, well after hostilities had ceased. Many of these men were serving in the Royal Army Medical Corps, which suggests that Graham is correct.

Major Verschoyle Crawford Climo, who served with the Manchester Regiment and was a General Staff Officer, died of pneumonia after catching the Spanish 'Flu. He died aged 51 on 19 February 1919, and is buried with his parents in Yateley churchyard. His father, retired surgeon Lieutenant Colonel William Hill-Climo, was buried in the same grave on 25 July. The colonel and his wife, Margaret, had lived during the war at Fir Glen near the junction of Mill Lane and Chandlers Lane.

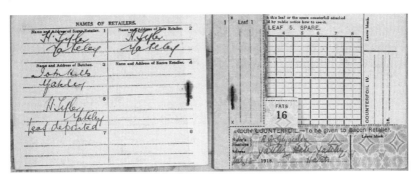

The ration book of Ena Guggisberg is stuck into the wartime scrapbook along with her sister's. It shows that Yateley Hall bought their meat from John Hill, behind the Dog & Partridge. The groceries came from Tyler's Store, the shop at the junction of Plough Lane and Blackwater Road. (Richard Johnston)

Armistice Day

Sydney Loader wrote in his memoirs:

'In November 1918 on the eleventh day of the eleventh month, at eleven a.m. the war ended, with the Armistice being signed. The house bell on the [Minley] manor [where he was

working as a gardener] was rung for a long time until the
rope broke, and everyone went home for the rest of the day.
It was such a relief, for the casualties had been so heavy and
most families had lost someone.'

The Spring 1919 Electoral Registers recorded the names of 246
male residents of Yateley still away from home – almost exactly a
quarter of all those then living in the civil parish registered to vote
in parliamentary elections. This number does not, of course, include
all those who had been killed. The full story would not even be told
by the addition of those killed to this number of registered voters.
Of the fifty-seven men named in the *Hants & Berks Gazette* Roll of
Honour at Christmas 1914, eight were dead, but only thirty more
were registered to vote in January 1919. The population remained
fluid throughout the war.

The exact numbers of men serving depends on how closely we
define their connection with Yateley. There were 402 men whose
names were included in the *Hants & Berks Gazette*; the St Peter's
and Scout rolls of honour; the 1918 or 1919 Electoral Registers;
Yateley Village School registers; were married in Yateley during the
war, or whose names were inscribed on the Yateley War memorial.
There were at least as many men who served in the Great War as
there were numbers of houses in Yateley. The number of inhabited
houses grew from 440 in 1911 to 481 in 1921.

In November 1918, Sybil Howell was in London attending
lectures on massage to retake the exam she had previously failed
to pass. Her graphic eyewitness account of London at the end of
the war is recorded in her diary, starting with her entry for Monday
11 November 1918:

'War has stopped! 11 AM. We all fled from the lecture room
into the Strand. Climbed up the steps of Nelson's Column.
Marched up the Mall. Mounted the Victoria Memorial.
Had splendid view of the Palace, the Royal Family. Massed
bands were splendid. The crowd fell on London with a yell,
and pandemonium reigned undisturbed. Got some lunch

307035 Private Edward N. Cooper MM
2/8th Royal Warwickshire Regiment
(London Gazette 19th March 1918 page 3461)

The four medals of Edward Nobes Cooper are in the museum of the Royal Warwickshire Regiment, the last regiment in which he served during the First World War. Private Cooper won the Military Medal for bravery, which is shown on the left. Next is the British War Medal, mainly awarded to those who served overseas, and the third is the Victory Medal, awarded to those who had entered a 'theatre of war' The medal on the far right is the Second World War Defence Medal. Edward Nobes Cooper served in the Yateley company of the Home Guard during the Second World War, when he lived at 6 Council Houses, Vigo Lane. During the First World War his home was in Eversley Lane, Yateley. (Royal Warwicks Museum)

at Victoria Station. Went to Thanksgiving Service at Abbey. The bells! The bells! Chiming and firing were too much for us. Sat next to the wireless engineer of Nansen's [sic, it was Amundsen's] crew in Australian uniform with white ribbon of South Polar Expedition ... of 1911-1913. Walked to ... from Abbey. Wet through. Felt tired.'

On the following day she continued:

'We decked the balcony with flags. I went off to massage class. We couldn't settle down. So went out into the Strand and saw King and Queen, Princess Patricia etc. driving in

State to St Paul's. Queen looked awfully well in red velvet and fur. Managed to fight into a No.11 and got home at 1. Wrote to Auntie May [the wife of the vicar of Yateley, and] Dorothy M [Macrae, Yateley's scout mistress]. Had a letter from Honor Blackden [of Byways, Vigo Lane]. My cold and cough still bad. Very foggy.'

Children's Christmas Party

A very special children's party was held in Yateley's Drill Hall for Christmas 1918. Herman Darewski had sent down from London a conjurer and a toy for each child. Darewski was a very successful composer and band leader who wrote music for popular songs. In 1914, he had written the music for *'Sister Susie's Sewing Shirts for Soldiers'*. He composed a number of musical revues, a new theatrical form which emerged in London during the First World War: *Business as Usual* (1914), *Push and Go* (1915), *Joyland* (1915), *Razzle Dazzle* (1916), *Carminetta* (1917) and *As you Were* (1918).

In 1917, he had composed the music for the hugely successful revue *The Better 'Ole, or the Romance of Old Bill*, which ran in London for 811 performances and was still running on Broadway during Christmas 1918, eventually completing 353 performances. In 1919, this 'smashing success' had opened in Chicago, Philadelphia, Boston and in Canada.

Herman Darewski was the son of a Russian emigré who had been a professor of music in Minsk. The family came to London when Herman was 13. He studied music in Vienna and at the London College of Music. In 1914, he married Madge Temple, the famous musical comedy actress. After Dr Petrie's death in 1917, the Darewskis had come to live at Barclay House in Yateley, probably to avoid the bombing in London.

Yateley's children would not get their fathers back until well into 1919, but at least 1918 would end on a high note for them at their Christmas party – effectively putting a full stop behind the war for them.

Aftermath

At the end of the Second World War, the people of Britain voted for a Government which would provide them with a better life. At the end of the Great War, what did the residents of Yateley want? Did they want the Government to reward them for all the heartbreak and hardships they had endured? Or did they expect to have to seek that better life for themselves? Did they want to go back to what it was like before the war? Or did they expect that the new technologies and medical advances, wrought during the war for the military, would provide them with a better life? Without a parish magazine, letters and diaries for Yateley, there are few clues as to what people were thinking. We can only judge by their actions. And it seems that different people answered all these questions in different ways; some, for example, by emigrating.

The people of Eversley, the next-door parish, knew one thing they wanted, and that was to reaffirm the values of Charles Kingsley. They decided to celebrate the centenary of Kingsley's birth by staging an enormous open-air pageant on the Mount overlooking the Rectory and St Mary's Church. The cast included almost the entire population of Eversley, as well as prestigious London artists. As the audience was over 3,000 for each of the three days, most of Yateley must have attended. The *Morning Post* declared: 'The Pageant was in perfect harmony with its setting, with the old-world peace and beauty of Eversley.'

The Eversley pageant was held at Whitsun 1919 before the village joined in the national Peace Day Celebrations on Saturday 19 July, and before its Dinner for Returned Soldiers in August. Yateley too held its celebrations on Peace Day, along with the rest of the country. The reason why a Bank Holiday was not declared until July was that the Treaty of Versailles was not signed until 19 June.

Kingsley Pageant *Eversley 1919*

In commemoration of the centenary of the birth of Charles Kingsley – the clergyman and writer of The Water-Babies *and* Westward Ho! *who was Rector of St Mary's Church in Eversley a large pageant was staged over three days in Eversley on the Mount in front of Eversley Rectory. Attended by over 9,000 spectators, practically everyone in Eversley took part. Held in Whit week 1919, the pageant preceded the national Peace Day. Vickers provided airplanes and pilots for joyrides. (Philip Todd)*

Peace Day was declared as a national holiday on 19 July 1919. Miss de Winton Corry organized the Yateley event. A large procession went down the Blackwater Road to Frogmore, then came back via Frogmore Road and Darby Green. This photograph from the Stilwell family album shows Miss Sybil Howell in fancy dress on the cart. She had been one of the crowd outside Buckingham Palace on 11 November 1918, Armistice Day. (Yateley Society Archive)

Miss de Winton Corry was the main organizer of Yateley's celebration. There were competitions for fancy dress and decorated floats. A full procession of all competitors set out from Yateley Hall, headed by a band. The route went down the main road towards Blackwater, turned into Frogmore Road, returned through Frogmore and Darby Green, and arrived back for a free tea in the marquees erected in Yateley Hall park. Tea was followed by sports events and then a bonfire and dancing on Yateley Green.

The three young daughters of Fred and Nellie Bull dressed up as VADs. Nellie was one of Yateley's letter carriers, and Frederick Charles Bull had been a farrier-sergeant in the Army Veterinary Corps. When he was de-mobbed, he found it difficult to find a job as a blacksmith. Most of the local gentry had now acquired motor cars. Nellie was a Sandhurst girl, and her sister, Margaret, had married a Canadian serviceman, Francis Leonard Vaness, in Sandhurst in 1917. He persuaded Fred there were still opportunities for blacksmiths in Canada. So Fred emigrated in 1920, ending up in Nipawin, Saskatchewan, working with Frank Vaness, who was the blacksmith there.

The three daughters of Fred and Nellie Bull all dressed up to enter the Yateley fancy dress competition on Peace Day, 19 July 1919. They were granddaughters of Annie Bull, for many years one of Yateley's letter carriers, and daughters of Fred Bull, the blacksmith who had emigrated to Canada. (Linda Davis)

This receipt from the Bull family archive is dated 22 October 1922. It confirms that Fred Bull had made an application for land to build a homestead in Nipawin on the Saskatchewan River in Canada, and paid the $10 fee to the Canadian authorities. Nipawin was first settled as a trading post in 1910, and was about 225 miles north of the Canadian Pacific railway passing through Regina, Saskatchewan. In 1924, a railway was built near Nipawin and the settlement moved to the new station. Fred became the blacksmith there, but his brother-in-law remained in the original settlement. (Linda Davis)

Their business must have prospered, as Fred sent for his wife and children in 1922, and his mother and half-sister in 1924. The winter temperature in Nipawin dropped to minus 40° in those days.

Another Canadian town which experienced similar low temperatures was Chicoutimi, on the Saguenay River in the Province of Quebec. In 1924, Jack Stilwell emigrated to an office job there with Price Brothers Limited, a major logging company and pulp and paper producer. Jack had to resign before he had been there three years 'on account of the climatic conditions in Canada'. Captain John Grant Stilwell had lost a lung when he was wounded in Mesopotamia. He spent the remainder of the war as a prisoner in Turkey. In Chicoutimi, he probably found it difficult breathing at such low temperatures.

'This is Fred Bull with children Marjorie (Queenie), my mother, and George, her brother who died of diphtheria. My mother sailed from England in May 1922 with her mother, grandmother and siblings so I expect this photo was taken shortly after their arrival in Nipawin, or perhaps that autumn. You can see how rustic the surroundings are. Quite the contrast to Yateley – brave souls!' (photograph and caption courtesy of Linda Davis, Canada, a descendant)

Whilst some people were emigrating from Yateley, newcomers were buying homes here. Many were retired high-ranking army officers. Before the war ended, Major-General Robert Hunter Murray CB CMG had moved into the Red House on Hall Lane, next door to Colonel Eustace Edward Melville Lawford, who had changed his house name from Holmdene to Yateley Court. General Murray held the ceremonial rank of Colonel of the Regiment of the Seaforth Highlanders from 1914 until his death in 1925, and had been Aide-de-Camp to Queen Victoria.

Another newcomer was Frank Currie Lowis, a colonel in the Indian Army. He purchased Monteagle Farm in 1920 from Major Alexis Doxat VC. Colonel Lowis was a grandson of Sir Frederick Currie, the last Chairman of The Honourable East India Company, before it was nationalized in 1858. Lowis had strong local connections. Sir Frederick, a cousin of Raikes Currie who built

The Red House, now demolished, stood on Hall Lane where Willowford is today, next door to Yateley Court. In 1915, the Red House had been the home of Major Villiers Riall, but by 1918 Major General Robert Hunter Murray and his wife, Florence Elizabeth Catherine, had moved in. There are several photographs of him in the National Portrait Gallery and the Royal Collection in the full dress uniform of the Seaforth Highlanders. This photograph of the Red House was taken in 1892. (From an auction document in the Yateley Society Archive).

Minley Manor, had not lived in Yateley, but his widow came to live at Holmdene, and she was buried in 1909 in St Peter's churchyard. One of Sir Frederick's daughters, Mabel Thornton Currie, was living in Up Green with Mrs Ada Verini. One of Sir Frederick's granddaughters was the wife of the Rev Tanner, the new Rector of Eversley. Another granddaughter was the wife of Lieutenant Colonel Bernard Stilwell, who had commanded the 2nd/4th Hampshire Regiment.

Look closely and you can find a family relationship between many of the main players in this story.

Having close relations in Yateley, and the proximity of Sandhurst, Aldershot and the Staff College in Camberley, might explain the influx of retired army officers. It is more difficult to explain why high-ranking naval officers retired here. James Rose Price Hawksley was a Welshman, and a hero of the Battle of Jutland,

This photograph of Monteagle House was taken by Sir Thomas Sturmy Cave on 29 July 1922. Two years earlier, the house had been bought from Major Alexis Charles Doxat VC by Colonel Frank Currie Lowis, when the latter retired from the Indian Army. The picture clearly shows that Lowis had recently replaced the outshut with a two-storey extension to include a new staircase and extra bedrooms. Colonel Cave had been visiting the house where his direct ancestor, William Cave, had added the porch in 1619, dying there in 1629. The house is now Grade II listed. (Richard Johnston)

having commanded the 11th Destroyer Flotilla Battle Fleet from HMS *Castor*. Like Colonels Lowis and Murray, he was listed in the 1919 edition of *Who's Who*, giving his rank of as commodore and address, HMS *Adventure*. Hawksley was promoted to rear-admiral on 23 July 1922, and was placed on the Retired List the next day at his own request. He and his wife appeared in the spring 1923 Yateley Electoral Register living at Heathcroft, which they had bought from the Mastermans.

Amongst other military newcomers was Lieutenant Commander Percy Hubert Boulnois, a wartime submarine commander. He arrived from Gosport with his wife in late 1920 to live at Yateley Lodge.

Cricket Hill Cottage on Cricket Hill became the home of Mrs Jessie Brown after the First World War. She was the widow of Colonel F.D.M. Brown, who was awarded the VC during the Indian Mutiny. She was the mother of Jessie Brown, the orthopaedic sister in the Great War who started Yateley Textiles, and of General Llewellyn Brown, interned at Ruhleben during the First World War, who became Director General of the Ordnance Survey. During the war the house was known as St George's. At the turn of the century it had been a girls' school, run by Mrs Wilding, where the war artist Paul Nash had been a pupil in the 1890s. (Malcolm Miller)

Homes For Heroes

For the first time, local authorities were given responsibility for building and government subsidies to finance working-class housing. The Housing, Town Planning, &c. Act 1919 aimed to provide half a million houses within three years, but ended up building fewer than half that number. The Hartley Wintney Rural District Council tried to do its bit. The Council purchased land from J.P. Stilwell on 15 September 1920. The site, part of Moor Place Farm, was a field facing Yateley Green on the north side of Vicarage Road.

The spring 1923 Electoral Register shows that all twelve semi-detached homes had been built, naming them New Cottages. In the Electoral Registers immediately before and after the Second World War, some are named Council Cottages, Yateley Green and some are called Council Houses. All are given their numbers 1-12.

The occupants of numbers 8, 9 and 10 were the same in 1945 as they were in 1923, surnamed Piers, Sharp and Wheeler respectively.

Were they all 'Heroes', and were they Yateley 'Heroes'? Charles Wheeler at No.10 was certainly both. He was the man who had appealed unsuccessfully at the Military Tribunal in 1916. Born, married and buried in Yateley, he was the son of the 76-year-old farmer at Dungell's Farm, and had served in the 4th Hants from 1916. Another new occupant of the 'Homes for Heroes' was George Henry Greaves. After his father had appealed unsuccessfully at the Military Tribunals, he had served in the Army Service Corps from April 1917. John Adam North was a bricklayer living at Starve Acre when he had joined the Royal Flying Corps in 1916. Leading Telegraphist Clifford George Sealy, the son of the Stilwells' coachman, has come into our story several times. All these four men were recorded in 1919 as Absent Voters, still away doing military service.

None of the council tenants in any of the other eight houses lived in Yateley in 1919, and were unlikely to have ever lived here before they were given a Home for Heroes. George Halley Brown was one of the new council tenants who had been of military age during the war. In 1922, he had been living in Easton-on-the-Hill, a small village at the north-eastern tip of Northamptonshire. He had appeared before the Northamptonshire Military Tribunal on 10 October 1916, obtaining temporary deferment until 1 February 1917. On 6 June 1917, he was given an extension to 1 November 1917 as he was the head forester of a 2,510 acre woodland estate. It is not clear why he wanted to live in Yateley in 1923, nor what criteria Hartley Wintney RDC used for allocating the twelve new council houses. Perhaps allocations were made nationally, as there seems to have been no preference for local people or local heroes.

Remembrance

Kelly's Directorty of 1923 states:

> *'Opposite the church, on land presented by the Misses Mason, is a Calvary raised on a base of four pedestals, two rough unhewn, the two others polished. At the base is inscribed "To the memory*

*of the men of Yateley who fell in the Great War, 1914-1919.
Grant them, O lord, eternal rest. Greater love hath no man
than this, that a man lay down his life for his friends." The cost
was £350, raised by public subscription, and the memorial was
unveiled in April, 1920, by General Horne G.G.B., K.C.M.G.'*

Surprisingly, the subject of the war is hardly mentioned in the
minutes of the Parish Council throughout its duration. The small
committee set up to raise the money to erect the War Memorial
were all members of St Peter's Church. It is not therefore surprising
that the memorial does not cover the whole of the Civil Parish of
Yateley. The Parish Council only took over the maintenance of the
memorial in 1936 after all the Misses Mason had died. The land
on which the Yateley memorial stands was donated to the church,
consecrated at the unveiling ceremony and is still consecrated.

*The Rev George Herbert Oakshott reads out the forty-two names on the Roll of
Honour at the unveiling and dedication of the Yateley War Memorial. He had served
as a chaplain in the Royal Navy at Gallipoli, and later at Chatham. General Lord
Horne GCB KCMG performed the unveiling. (Jean McIlwaine)*

The reasons why a name may or may not have been recorded on a village war memorial are complex. We have found twenty-seven servicemen who were born in the Civil Parish of Yateley and lost their lives during the First World War, only fifteen of whom are named on the Yateley War Memorial. As we have shown, this is partly because the Yateley memorial was erected to record the names of the relatives of families living in the ecclesiastical parish of St Peter's. Of the twenty-eight men born here, eight are remembered at Hawley Memorial Hall. Although they lived in the Yateley Civil Parish, they lived in Frogmore, which was part of the large ecclesiastical parish of Holy Trinity Hawley. Of the remaining men born in Yateley but are not on the War Memorial, most attended Yateley's village school, but their families had left the village before the end of the war.

Before and during the Great War, Yateley was a village with a large transient population. We can therefore expect that the families of many of the dead men would either have arrived in Yateley in the fifteen years of housing expansion before the war or left before the end of the war. We have compiled a list of seventy-eight men having some sort of connection with Yateley. Their deaths were all war related within the period defined by the Commonwealth War Graves Commission.

One way to investigate these men and the families they left behind is to look in the 1918 Electoral Register to see in which ecclesiastical parish they lived. Of these eighty men, 49 per cent (thirty-nine) had a parent or wife living in 1918 in the parish of St Peter's Yateley, fifteen families lived in Holy Trinity Hawley and five lived in St Mary's Eversley. This means that the families of almost a quarter of these men did not live in any of these three Church of England parishes on 15 July 1918, the date of the Register. But all these men had been born or married here. It is not therefore surprising that the forty-two names on the Yateley War Memorial do not tell the whole story of the village in the Great War.

Some men left behind them very special memorials in flesh and blood, bearing their own name. We have already told how sons were named exactly for John Archibald Ainslie and Herbert Clifford Larder. Archie Goodall's wife had her husband's posthumous daughter baptized Gwendolen Archie. One of the first men to die

Yateley Church War Memorial.

Unveiling and Dedication Service,

SATURDAY, FEBRUARY 25th, 1922, at 3 p.m.

✠

1914—1919.

TO THE GLORY OF
GOD & IN MEMORY
OF THE MEN FROM
THIS PARISH WHO
MADE THE SUPREME
SACRIFICE FOR GOD
& KING FOR FREEDOM
RIGHT AND PEACE
IN THE GREAT WAR.

"By the long road they trod
with so much faith and with
such devoted and self-sacri-
ficing bravery we have arrived
at Victory and to-day they
have their reward."

F.-M. Earl Haig's last Despatch.

WILLIAM ABERY.
JOHN A. AINSLIE.
PERCY ALDERMAN.
HERBERT BACKHURST.
WILFRID BLACKDEN.
ALFRED BLACKMAN.
GEORGE BRENCH.
WYNYARD K. BROWN.
BERT BUNCH.
CHARLES BUTLER.
HENRY COTTERILL.
FREDERICK DAVIS.
ARCHIBALD GOODALL.
FREDERICK GRAINGER.
MARK HAMMOND.
GEORGE HARRIS.
HENRY HARRIS.
ARTHUR HARRISON.
WILLIAM HEARMON.
JOHN HICKS.

THOMAS W. HICKS.
REGINALD F. HICKS.
ROBERT W. HOILE.
HARRY HOOPER.
JAMES A. HORNE.
WILLIAM HUDSON.
CECIL H. KER.
ARTHUR LARDER.
CLARENCE R. LEGG.
REGINALD LEGG.
CHARLES M. MACRAE.
WILFRED MAYBANKS.
JOHN C. MILLS.
ARTHUR MUSTOW.
JAMES H. SILLENCE.
HERBERT STOOKS.
BERTIE L. VOKES.
LLOYD WHEELER.
FRANK WINCH.
CHARLES WOOLDRIDGE.

A. J. HOWELL, M.A., *Vicar.*

E. E. M. LAWFORD, Colonel, ⎫
B. E. CAREY, O.B.E., ⎬ *Churchwardens.*
⎭

The sheet produced for the service on 25 February 1922 to unveil and dedicate the war memorial in the chancel of St Peter's church. The names of men honoured are almost identical to the names on the public war memorial unveiled two years earlier. The original stone memorial in the chancel was so badly damaged when the church was destroyed by arson in 1979 that it has been replaced by a memorial in wood with gold lettering. (Richard Johnston)

in the Great War was Rifleman William Arthur Lawrence, serving with the Kings Royal Rifles. His wife, Eva, baptized her son William Henry and the Vicar wrote in the Burial Register after the father's name 'K.R.R. (Deceased)'.

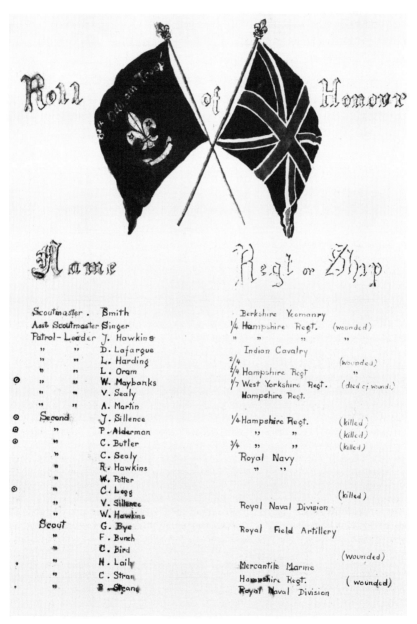

Roll of Honour

Name	Regt or Ship
Scoutmaster . Smith	Berkshire Yeomanry
Asst Scoutmaster Singer	¼ Hampshire Regt. (wounded)
Patrol – Leader J. Hawkins	" " "
" " D. Lafargue	Indian Cavalry
" " L. Harding	2/4 (wounded)
" " L. Oram	2/4 Hampshire Regt "
○ " " W. Maybanks	1/7 West Yorkshire Regt. (died of wounds)
" " V. Sealy	Hampshire Regt.
" " A. Martin	
○ Second J. Sillence	¼ Hampshire Regt. (killed)
○ " P. Alderman	" " (killed)
○ " C. Butler	3/4 " " (killed)
" C. Sealy	Royal Navy
" R. Hawkins	" "
" W. Potter	
○ " C. Legg	(killed)
" V. Sillence	Royal Naval Division
" W. Hawkins	
Scout G. Bye	Royal Field Artillery
" F. Bunch	
" C. Bird	(wounded)
" H. Laily	Mercantile Marine
" C. Stran	Hampshire Regt. (wounded)
" B. Sloane	Royal Naval Division

There are twenty-four names on the Roll of Honour of the Yateley Scouts. It lists the scoutmaster, his assistant, seven patrol leaders, nine seconders and six scouts. Of the men honoured, five were killed and six more wounded – almost half were in the thick of battle and paid the price. (Peter Tipton)

Interwar Social Changes

The First World War panels on the Yateley War Memorial name only two officers who actually lived in Yateley on 5 August 1914, one a reservist the other a territorial. The percentage of all nine officers to 'other ranks' on the Great War panels is 21 per cent, whereas on the Second World War panels the ratio of officers is 60 per cent. During the Second World War, one-third of the officers killed were serving with the Indian Army. The marked difference between these two memorials reflects the social change in Yateley in the interwar years.

The list of 'Private Residents' in Yateley in the 1915 edition of *Kelly's Directory* gives the names of fifty-six people, of whom twenty-nine (52 per cent) were female. Of these fifty-six, only three have an entry in *Who's Who*: Brigadier-General William Johnson Kirkpatrick CB, Sir Charles Stewart-Wilson KCIE and Colonel Alexander William Macrae. In contrast, *Kelly's* in 1939 contains seventy-six names, of which twelve were included in the 1939 edition of *Who's Who*.

The late Mrs Ena Louise Collison, owner of Tice's Stores and Chaddisbrooke from 1934, recalled:

> '*Yateley was a true village until after the war ... Most people were retired and the few 'natives' earned a living cleaning, cooking and gardening for the 'gentry', many of whom already employed full time live-in cooks and housekeepers. If one by any chance saw a pram there would be a uniformed nurse pushing it.*'

Kelly's Directories divide the population into two categories, the gentry and commercial, leaving the rest unnamed. There was no census in 1941, so we have to rely on population statistics for 1931, roughly halfway through the interwar period. To obtain a fuller picture of the changing social hierarchy, we can consult the *Kelly's* 1931 edition. The number of gentry listed had already increased to seventy-four, from the fifty-six in 1915. The fifty-nine commercial residents in 1931 had increased in number from twenty-two. *Kelly's* thus listed 22 per cent of Yateley's households in 1931, giving a picture of the main characteristics of the total 617 households.

During the interwar years, most new housing estates built in Yateley were council houses. After the Homes for Heroes were built, three more council estates followed, at Little Vigo, Bell Lane and Moulsham Copse, enabling many of the artisans, builder's labourers, gardeners and errand boys who had fought in the war to move into modern housing.

As well as the new council houses being built, old farmhouses and artisan cottages were being gentrified as homes for the gentry newcomers to Yateley. Two-thirds of the male 'private residents' in 1931 were listed in *Kelly's* by their military rank. It would be mostly their sons, and the sons of First World War war-widows, who would be the officers who represented 60 per cent of the names on the Second World War panels of the Yateley War Memorial.

During the First World War, this house was called Fir Glen and was the home of Lieutenant Colonel William Hill Climo and his wife, Margaret Jane. Colonel Hill Climo had retired in 1893 as brigade-surgeon in the RAMC. He died in 1919, a few months after his son, Major Verschoyle Crawford Climo, died of Spanish flu whilst still serving. When Margaret Hill Climo died in 1922, the house was sold to Mrs Hetty Rose, the war widow of Captain Ronald Hugh Walrond Rose, killed on 22 October 1914. She renamed the house The Paddock, after her previous house in Heston in the Wirral. The house was built by Bertie Fullbrook, who had lived in it himself in 1912. It was demolished after the Second World War. (Rose family album)

After the Second World War, it would be the large houses of the gentry which were demolished to make room for the new housing estates, changing the character of Yateley yet again, and increasing its population tenfold from what it had been at the end of the First World War. The only reminders of the houses, gardens, parkland and families which played such an essential part in the Great War are street names in the new housing estates such as Byways, Coleridge Avenue, Firglen Drive, Frogmore Park Road, Hall Farm Crescent, Harpton Parade, Hearmon Close, Hilfield, Ives Close, Macrae Road, Manor Park Drive, Mason Close, Robins Grove Crescent, Stilwell Close and White House Gardens.

Bibliography

Published books

Baigent, Francis Joseph, *The Crondal Records Part 1, Historical and Manorial*, Hampshire Record Society (London, Simpkin & Co, 1891).

Beckett, Ian F.W., *Riflemen Form: A Study of the Rifle Volunteer Movement 1859-1908* (Barnsley, Pen & Sword Books, 1982), Kindle Edition.

Beckett, Ian F.W., *The Making of the First World War* (New Haven, Conn, Yale University Press, 2012).

Cave, Thomas Sturmy, *History of the First Volunteer Battalion Hampshire Regiment, 1859 to 1889. With appendix containing notes and illustrations in reference to the corps from 1890 to 1903* (London, Simpkin & Co., 1905).

Fitzroy, Yvonne, *With the Scottish Nurses in Roumania* (London, John Murray, 1918; reprinted Oakpast Ltd, 2013).

Fletcher, Anthony, *Life, Death and Growing Up on the Western Front* (New Haven, Conn, Yale University Press, 2013).

Fleuty, Graham, *Yateley Men at War, Heartbeats of Remembrance* (Chichester, Phillimore, 2011).

Floate, Sharon Sillers, *My Ancestors were Gypsies* (London, Society of Genealogists, 2010), Kindle Edition.

Hanson, Neil, *Priestley's Wars* (Bradford, Great Northern Books, 2008), pp.31-32.

Page, William (ed.), *A History of the County of Hampshire: Volume 4* (London, Victoria County History, 1911).

Stilwell, John Bernard L, *The Tiger*, magazine of the 4th Hampshire Regiment, 1915.

Stooks, Rev Charles Drummond, *A History of Crondall & Yateley* (Winchester, Warren & Son, 1903).

Hampshire Record Office, Winchester

Muster Rolls for Crondall Hundred, 1 September 1925, HRO 44M69/G5/26/4.

Records of Yateley Village School 1865 to 1918, HRO 64M83.

Homes for Heroes: title deeds to land at Vicarage Road, Yateley, purchased by Hartley Wintney RDC from J.P. Stilwell 1920, HRO 52/M97/T31.

Yateley War Memorial: conveyance of land by gift and other correspondence 1920-1939, HRO 44M68/F2/484.

Electoral Registers for Yateley: Basingstoke H/CL9/4/97 (1914); Aldershot H/CL9/4/19-38 (1918-1930); Aldershot H/CL9/4/47 (1939) and H/CL9/4/47 (1945).

'Voluntary Aid Organisations in Hampshire', final report of Hampshire Red Cross 1919, HRO 173A12/A1/2/1.

The National Archives, Kew

Land Tax Assessments for Yateley IR58/5268, 5270, 5271, 5272, 5273, 5274, 5275, 5276, 5277, 5278, 34438, 34439, 34440, 52332.

Ministry of Health, War Refugees Committee: Minutes, Papers and History Cards, Belgian Refugee History Cards (1914-1918), Boxes MH 8/39 to MH/92.

Other Archives

Lothian Health Service Archives, University of Edinburgh Library, Copy letterbooks Yvonne Fitzroy (1916-17) LHB8/6-7; Scrapbook of Yvonne Fitzroy LHB8/12/8.

General Registry Office certificates

When the event was not in Yateley, we have purchased nineteen birth, marriage and death certificates where they would contribute significantly to our story.

Newspapers
Various newspapers, magazines and journals – particularly the *Reading Mercury*, *Hants & Berks Gazette*, *Camberley News*, *The Times*, the *London Gazette*, the *Journal of the Royal College of Nursing* and the *Eversley Parish Magazine* – have been consulted in various locations and media, including at Surrey Heath Museum, Basingstoke Discovery Centre, Hampshire Library & Archives and online via Hampshire Library Service, FindMyPast and directly.

Directories
Kelly's Directories for 1911, 1912, 1915, 1920, 1923, 1925, 1929, 1935 and 1939 have been consulted either online, on purchased CD-ROM or in various archives; a printed copy of *Who's Who 1919* and *Who Was Who* online via Hampshire Library Service.

Personal Archives
We are indebted to many families, too numerous to mention individually, for assisting our research. We particularly thank those who have allowed us to quote from documents and use images as illustrations: Chris Bunch for the quotation from *The Tiger*, the magazine of the 4th Battalion, Hampshire Regiment and photographs; Yvonne Allen for key photographs; and Linda Davis for sending pictures and documents from Canada.

Yateley Society Digital Archives
Collison, Ena, notes re purchasing and running Tice's Stores before the Second World War.

Guggisberg, Ena & Nancy, scrapbook of photographs, cuttings, programmes etc. covering the First World War.

Harland, Gordon, handwritten notes of interview with Sam Chesterton, 13 May 1986.

Howell, Sybil, diary, handwritten in Army & Navy printed diary, 1918.

Ives, George, 'A Walk in the Past 1894-1970', unpublished typescript, 1970.

Kerslake, Valerie, oral history notes, mostly handwritten, various dates post-1976.

Loader, Sydney, 'The Changing Scene', unpublished typescript and drawings, 1981.

Stilwell, Norah et al, *Beatrice Ellen Stilwell, an appreciation by those with whom she worked and joined in sport*, privately published, 1933.

Stilwell, Norah G., 'Clooty', the story of her pet dog, unpublished typescript, including pasted-in photographs and postcards.

Tice, William Burroughs, handwritten pocket book covering First World War dates.

Whitehorn, John Parker, correspondence with Sydney Loader.

Yateley Midwifery Register of Cases, home visits with medical details 1908-1922.

The Yateley Society has deposited all its physical archive at Hampshire Record Office, ref. 186A09. The Society has also contributed over 100 digital images to the Hampshire Photographic Collection HPP61/001-101.

To enable the Society to trace the existence of, and the owners and occupiers of Yateley's heritage assets from before 1700, its archive contains a digital transcription of the manorial court books, all published census records, the taxation records, marriages, baptisms and burials, plus copies of the tithe map and all large-scale Ordnance Survey maps before 1939. All have been used for this book.

Research for the two 'virtual walks' on 27 January 1916 and 15 July 1918 has been greatly facilitated by a digital interactive map of Yateley created by Chris Willis from transcript and photographs of the 1910 Land Tax Assessment at The National Archives, Kew, made by Richard Johnston, combined with databases of electoral registers for 1914, 1918 and 1919 created from transcripts made by Chris Willis and Peter Tipton at Hampshire Record Office in Winchester.

Imperial War Museum: Lives of the Great War
The Imperial War Museum has created a permanent digital memorial to all those persons from throughout the Commonwealth who served

in the Great War. The *Yateley Community* on 'LivesOfWW1' is the permanent memorial to all those Yateley men and women who served in uniform in the Great War, whether they died or survived. The 'Life Story' page for each person connects with their military, civil and family records to create their life story as their memorial. If you do not find mention of your relative in this book, then you should find him or her at https://livesofthefirstworldwar.org/community/264. Creating the *Yateley Community* at 'LivesOfWW1' has been an invaluable research tool for this book.

Index